The Challenge of Toddlers

The Challenge of Toddlers

— For Teen Parents —

Parenting Your Child from One to Three

Jeanne Warren Lindsay, MA, CFCS

Morning
Glory
Press

Buena Park, California

The Challenge of Toddlers
is part of the five-book *Teens Parenting* series. Other titles are:

Your Pregnancy and Newborn Journey: A Guide for Pregnant Teens

Your Baby's First Year: A Guide for Teen Parents

***Discipline from Birth to Three: How Teen Parents Can Prevent and
Deal with Discipline Problems with Babies and Toddlers***

Teen Dads: Rights, Responsibilities and Joys

Library of Congress Cataloging-in-Publication Data
Lindsay, Jeanne Warren.
    The Challenge of Toddlers : for teen parents : parenting yor
child from one to three / Jeanne Warren Lindsay. -- Rev. ed.
        p.   cm. -- (Teens parenting)
    Includes bibliographical references and index.
    Summary: Describes for teenage parents the development and
special needs of children from one to three and offers advice and
comments from many young parents themselves.
    ISBN 1-885356-38-2. -- ISBN 1-885356-39-0 (Paper)
    1. Toddlers--United States--Juvenile literature. 2. Child rearing
--United Sates--Juvenile literature. 3. Teenage parents--United
States--Juvenile literature. [1. Teenage parents. 2. Parenting. 3.
Child development.] I. Title. II. Series: Lindsay, Jeanne Warren.
Teens parenting.
HQ774.5.L56 1998
649'. 122--dc21   98-35683
                                                        CIP
                                                         AC

MORNING GLORY PRESS, INC.
6595 San Haroldo Way   Buena Park, CA 90620-3748
714/828-1998   1-888/612-8254
Printed and bound in the United States of America

Contents

Preface   9

Foreword — Jan Stanton   11

Foreword — Lois H. Gatchell   13

1   **He's One — Soon He'll Be Running**   18
12-18 Months
  - Tremendous changes in both of you
  - Walking adds excitement • He jabbers before he talks • She copies Mom and Dad
  - Emotions develop rapidly • Your problem-solving toddler • From bottle or breast to cup
  - Helping baby's brain develop

2   **She's Struggling for Independence**   32
18-24 Months
  - Toddlers, like teenagers, struggle for independence
  - When your child asks for help • "Terrible Twos"
  - Her skills increase rapidly • Coping with fears
  - Don't rush toilet teaching • Major tasks for parents
  - Most important stage in life

3   Active Play — A Toddler's Work   42
       12-24 Months
       • Active play is valuable • Play ball!
       • Play space, play time needed • Play with him often
       • Classifying objects • Plan for indoor play
       • Making toys at home

4   Her Imagination Soars   56
       12-24 Months
       • She loves to pretend • Let him "help"
       • Toddlers and talking • Don't correct his speech
       • Read to your child • Choose non-sexist books
       • You're the teacher

5   Dad's Ahead If He's Involved   66
       12-36 Months
       • Some fathers are very involved
       • Others leave it up to Mom • Building a family
       • Learning to be a father • When Dad lives elsewhere
       • Maintaining a relationship
       • Your child changes your life

6   Mealtime for Toddlers   80
       12-36 Months
       • Keeping mealtime pleasant • She can eat with you
       • Offer small helpings • Coping with messiness
       • Toddler needs less food • Serving new foods
       • Outlaw junk food • Fat-proofing your toddler
       • Nutrition and extended family living
       • It's your responsibility

7   Importance of Sleep   96
       12-36 Months
       • Sleep/rest important for toddlers
       • Importance of bedtime ritual
       • Solving bedtime problems • She doesn't want to be
         alone • Every-five-minutes routine • Night waking
       • Should child sleep with parent? • Crowded home
         affects sleeping habits • Remember — routine helps

8   Your Amazing Two-Year-Old   110
  • New world of learning • Your child's first teacher
  • Read to him again and again • "I love you, Mommy"
  • To bed, to sleep? • No mealtime arguments
  • "Where do babies come from?" • Potty training
  • Hard to accept change • Even more patience needed
  • Winning — for both of you • You're his model

9   Playing with Your Two-Year-Old   124
  • Sometimes she's self-sufficient • Made-at-home toys
  • Time for finger painting • Teaching with games
  • Helping Mom and Dad • Celebrating holidays
  • How much television? • Select programs carefully
  • Playing outside • What about cold weather?
  • An athlete already?

10   Guarding Your Toddler's   140
       Health and Safety
  • Your toddler needs even more supervision
  • Protect him from burns • Poisoning is big danger
  • Cars can be deadly • Preventing serious illness
  • Your baby needs a doctor • Diarrhea still dangerous
  • When your child gets sick • Ear infection must be
    treated • Caring for toddler's teeth

11   Protecting Your Child from Sexual Abuse   154
  • Teen parents and sexual abuse • Sexual abuse is
    devastating • Protecting your children from abuse
  • Heart to Heart Program • Does abuse affect
    one's parenting? • "I finally told my mom"
  • Who do you tell? • Getting professional help

12   The Partnership Challenge   164
  • Parenting Alone • When you date again
  • Is marriage a solution? • Divorce is difficult
  • Making the marriage decision • Making a good
    partnership better • Winning over the other parents
  • Planning your family • What are your options?
  • Enough time for first child

13   Gang Involvement Versus Parenting   180
   • Pregnancy may be a way out
   • Does gang involvement affect parenting?
   • Why join a gang? • Gang clothes on babies?
   • Will your child join a gang? • Getting out

14   Your Future — Your Child's Future   196
   • Looking ahead • Taking financial responsibility
   • Importance of education • Non-traditional jobs
     for women • After high school, what?
   • Job helps self-esteem • Who stays home with
     the kids? • Heavy expense of moving out
   • Money versus happiness • When you have other
     problems • Finding community resources
   • Don't give up • Pregnancy and marital counseling
   • Writing your life script

Appendix   213

Bibliography   215

Index   221

Preface

If you've been a parent for at least a year, or if you will be the parent of a child aged one to three, this book is for you. It's especially for you if you're a teenage parent.

Teenage mothers and fathers share their parenting insights throughout these pages. They speak from their realities, the realities of teenagers who are also parents. They share their dreams and their frustrations, their hopes and fears for their children and themselves.

Child-rearing is not the only topic discussed in these chapters. Tips for meeting your own needs are also offered. One of the most important things you can do for your child is to make a satisfying life for yourself as well as for him/her. You'll be able to parent better if your own life is going well. Caring for an active toddler may make it harder for you to follow your dreams. That's why it's even more important for you to make a plan now to start working toward those goals and those dreams.

During your baby's first year, you were probably absorbed in childcare. Caring for your baby was an all-consuming task. Your personal needs may have received little attention.

By the time your baby is a year old, however, you may realize you need to get on with your own life, even as you continue caring for your child.

This book provides a guide for caring for children aged one to three years. It covers such topics as child development, nutrition, sleep, language development, health and safety, and activities for toddlers. Throughout, comments from young parents reinforce the concepts presented.

Other chapters focus on the needs of teen parents themselves. While the entire book is directed to both mothers and fathers, two chapters discuss two-parent issues specifically. "Dad's Ahead If He's Involved" advocates for strong two-parent cooperation in child-rearing when feasible, whether or not the parents are living together.

Teenage parents may be married to each other, they may be living together, be "together" but living apart, or one or both may be with a different partner. "The Partnership Challenge" provides a discussion of these various relationships. Young parents share insights gained from their experience with partners.

One of the two new chapters in this edition focuses on the impact on parenting of parents' gang involvement. The other is for young mothers who have had to cope with sexual and other abuse as they grew up, and on protecting one's child from abuse.

The final chapter provides suggestions for you as you plan your future life. The importance of continuing your education, obtaining job skills, and becoming independent is emphasized.

Parenting a toddler is a difficult task for parents of any age. Combine this task with the special needs of adolescents, and it becomes a gigantic challenge. I hope this book will help you in your quest for a satisfying life for yourself even as you parent your toddler.

Jeanne Warren Lindsay   August, 1998

Foreword

The primary focus of my work over the past decade has been developing programs and training professionals who work with teen parents. This work, as well as speaking with young parents, has prompted me to reflect on my thirty-year journey of parenting to draw on lessons learned. One of those reflections included the challenge of parenting for the first time. It was both frightening and rewarding. But somewhere between these two feelings we parents discover ourselves in the journey into a lifetime of parenthood — which, by the way, will be your most difficult journey in life.

The knowledge and support needed to be a good parent is an important part of this journey. This book is about that knowledge and support, and how to include the information in your daily life.

As your children start to explore their world, they will soon discover that a few steps away from you, their parents, is a whole new world waiting for them. They are just beginning to understand how big their world will eventually

become. It is difficult to believe that you cannot and will
not be with your children every moment of every day. You
want to learn and practice skills that better equip you to
make positive choices for yourself and for your children so
their world is a happier and safer one. One of the best ways
you can learn and practice the necessary skills to both
parent and to protect your child when they are not in your
care is to study the lessons presented in this book.

Throughout *The Challenge of Toddlers,* author Jeanne
Warren Lindsay has given you the knowledge to succeed
during your parenting journey. Each chapter takes you one
step closer to understanding the various aspects of
parenting and the challenges you face as you parent your
child from age one to three.

Pay special attention to the chapter on protecting your
child from sexual abuse. Like most young parents, we take
care to child-proof our homes. While we may child-proof
their immediate environment, we cannot protect our children from every harm. But we can take steps to protect our
young children from people who might harm them in some
way. Remember that not everyone loves your child the
same way you do, and some people believe that it is all
right to hurt children through abuse or neglect. No child,
especially your child, deserves to be hurt. Our children
deserve and need our respect in the same way we need and
deserve respect from others.

Whether the quotes from other teen parents say what is
on your mind, or the words of the author impress you, seek
the support of others during your journey through
parenting. Strong support through knowledge, friends, and
family will allow you to be the best parent that you can be.
Remember, our children deserve our best efforts.

Jan Stanton, Director   August, 1998
Heart to Heart

Foreword

I wish there had been a Jeanne Lindsay in my life in the late 1940s when I was having babies. Although I was a college graduate, married to a loving, supportive husband, I felt parenthood was the most important job I had ever undertaken, yet the one for which I was least prepared. I could have used the practical insights that Lindsay passes on to young parents that are reassuring, challenging, and fun.

Ideally, parenting should be enjoyed, as well as understood. This is not easy if the pregnancy was unplanned or unwanted. But the bond that a young woman usually begins to develop with the fetus becomes full blown when a new human being emerges from her labor.

Most of us can deal with the infant stage, because we love to feel needed. A cuddly infant is dependent, and gradually grows responsive to our display of affection — most rewarding! But when that infant turns into an active toddler with the curiosity of an explorer, the imagination of an artist, and the rebelliousness of an adolescent, watch out.

This is when the understanding, tact, challenge, patience, and yes, endurance, of mothers and fathers is summoned.

If we parents cultivate these characteristics, then we find the *joy* of watching a unique personality unfold before our eyes. With eyes to see and ears to hear, we are privileged to be part of the world of very interesting little people. This is apparent in Lindsay's book. Whether she is dealing with motor skills, feeding, bedtime, safety, active play, or planning for the future, there is the fun of the present developmental stage as well as the hope of the good life to come.

When I was director of the Margaret Hudson Program for teenage parents in Tulsa, Oklahoma, I found the fun of the hundreds of babies with whom we dealt was their differences. Surely there were common aspects of development, but also very early they had distinct personalities.

These babies enriched the parents, the staff, and each other as they learned to respond to their environment. We had the sense of being potters, experimenting with lumps of human clay. I, for one, would find myself praying to my God, "Oh, Lord, make me a worthy potter of this precious little vessel."

The teen mothers and fathers quoted in this book are confronting the realities of parenthood. One would hope that they, and those who come after, would find the supports in our society that provide the needed guidance and encouragement to produce competent, healthy children. *The Challenge of Toddlers* is one of these supports.

(The Reverend) Lois H. Gatchell
Deacon, Episcopal Diocese of Oklahoma

Acknowledgments

I am grateful to Sally and Stewart McCullough, Diane Smallwood, Jean Brunelli, Jan Stanton, Pat Alviso, and Pati Lindsay who made time to read and critique part or all of this revised edition, and to all those who read the earlier edition. Their comments were invaluable.

Perhaps even more important is the input from teen parents, the young people we interviewed, and whose wisdom is scattered throughout the book. For the first edition, 67 young people were quoted. For this revised edition, 54 more were interviewed, and many of this group are quoted here. They include Alysson Hall, Tim Whitehead, Andrea Gonzales, Carlos Smith, Antonee Williams, Brandi Hatch, Erika Madrid, Ernie Mejia, Gabriel Garcia, Priscilla Correa, Harmony Tortorice, Isabel Franco, Jessica Marquez, Juan Zepeda, Katie Stonebarger, Katrina Amaya, Laura Lilio, Laura Moran, Maria Almarez Valtierrez, Melisa Romero, Mira Montepio, Noel Mejia, Racheal Malonay, Robin Gardner, Robin Stanley, Rosa Paez, Shamika Mills, Stephanie Whittaker, Stormi Lopez, Tiffany Torres, Carlos Garcia, Tina Mondragon,

Veronica Bosquez, Yvette Aguirre, and Yolanda Torres. Others are quoted and acknowledged in the other books in the *Teens Parenting* series. We also appreciate the many other teenage parents whose insightful quotes are retained from the earlier edition.

David Crawford, teacher in the Teen Parent Program, William Daylor High School, Sacramento, supplied most of the photographs. His models were his wonderful students. A few other photos were contributed by Cheryl Boeller and Bob Lindsay.

Tim Rinker is the cover artist, and Steve Lindsay helped design the book. I am grateful for the contributions of all of these talented people.

Carole Blum and Karen Blake again helped with the proofreading and kept Morning Glory Press alive and well during book production time. I thank them for their valuable support.

Thank you, Bob, for being supportive and caring no matter what else is going on in our lives. I love you very.

Jeanne Lindsay
Buena Park, California

To the young parents who shared so freely
and taught me so much
as we worked together.

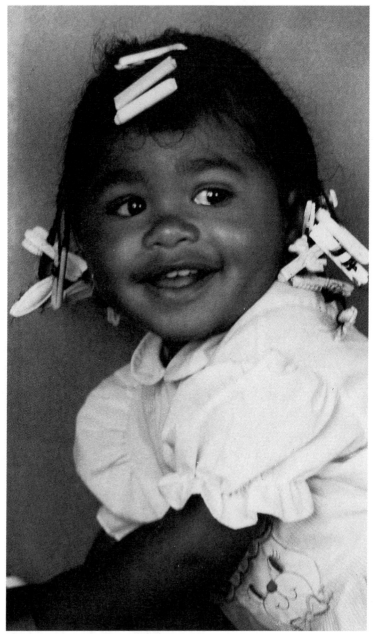

Your child is an exciting challenge.

1

He's One — Soon He'll Be Running

- **Tremendous Changesin Both of You**
- **Walking Adds Excitement**
- **He Jabbers Before He Talks**
- **She Copies Mom and Dad**
- **Emotions Develop Rapidly**
- **Your Problem-Solving Toddler**
- **From Bottle or Breast to Cup**
- **Helping Baby's Brain Develop**

Heidi loves to go to the park. She notices little bugs on the ground, little ants. She'll put her face down close to them, make her little noises, and show me.

She has a little bug catcher toy. When I put a bug in it, she picks it up and looks at it. Then I let the bug go.

I take her for a walk each evening. I teach her things on the way.

We stop every day and look at two dogs and some parakeets behind a fence down the street. One day the owner showed us his birds. She was thrilled.

Jenny, 18 - Heidi, 13 months

Tremendous Changes in Both of You

*Now Alice climbs off beds and is learning how to
climb up on the bed. I bought her a little skate toy
when she was one year old. Within a month, she
learned how to get on and off it. She also tried to stop
it from going anywhere by climbing on top of it.*

*She takes off her socks and shoes. She'll put her
shirt on. She likes to play peek-a-boo with it. If I'm
putting a shirt on, she'll pick up anything around,
maybe a nightgown, and put her head through the
hole. Then she laughs.*

Melanie, 15 - Alice, 13 months

At your child's first birthday you may be startled at the
changes you observe in each of you. Your child has developed from a helpless newborn to a whirlwind little person
who scoots everywhere and either is walking or will be
soon. Even more wonderful than his physical development
are the tremendous jumps in his knowledge. He's learning
many new things each day, and will continue to progress
rapidly with living, learning, and loving under your
guidance.

She is learning to walk, which gives her a lovely feeling
of independence. She can ride simple wheel toys. She's
discovered that by climbing she can find even more places
to explore. She can easily get herself into serious trouble if
no one is watching.

*Chandler climbs up on the rocking chair and onto
the end table. He'll go up on the couch and crawl all
the way up to the window. He will climb up a chair
with rungs until it falls over on him, but he's fine
when I take the chair off him.*

*He sits on my little sister's skateboard, and he
knows how to make it go.*

*Recently he started hitting. I tell him that hurts, and
I stop him.*

Gretchen, 17 - Chandler, 13 months

Your one-year-old has become more interested in toys
like shape boxes, formboards, blocks and balls. He especially enjoys these things if someone is nearby to watch or
play with him. He enjoys crayons or paints when he is
allowed to use them.

She is beginning to talk. She is learning to tell you what
she wants through words and gestures. She can follow
simple directions. But any understanding of right and
wrong, the ability to make simple judgments about behavior, will not even begin to emerge until she is close to two.
Even then she often won't know or understand what she
should or shouldn't do.

You, too, have probably changed a great deal during
your child's first year. Do you feel only a couple of years
older than you were BP (Before Pregnancy)? Or are you
convinced that you've grown up — matured — at a far
faster pace than your birthdays indicate? If you think
you're more mature than your actual years, you're probably
right. The responsibilities of parenting for both mothers and
fathers are awesome.

*The hardest part for me was the change when
Cassandra was born. I couldn't be myself anymore.
I couldn't stay young and irresponsible. It was hard
when we moved out when she was 14 months old. My
mother was always there doing stuff for me, and
Cassandra was in the infant center while I was
in school.*

*I didn't really have a chance to see what it was like
on my own until we moved. Her father helps me out,
but taking care of Cassie is still my responsibility. It's*

*also amazing how my love for her has grown since
I've been raising her on my own.*
Kris, 17 - Cassandra, 25 months

Perhaps the biggest change you'll experience with your
child during these toddler years is her individuality and
independence. When she was an infant, it was generally
your job to decide what was best for her. Now she will
insist more and more on making her own decisions.

Walking Adds Excitement

*Brandt walks everywhere. He doesn't want to
crawl any more. He walks all around the house, has
been for three weeks. He climbs on everything, the
chairs, up on the bed. He pushes the chair to the sink
and gets up there and plays with the water.*

*He throws his toys around and makes noises. He
pushes the little cars. He doesn't sit still, not even
when he's eating. He has to stand up and turn around.*
Sheleen, 15 - Brandt, 1

Once your baby starts walking, he's considered a toddler. Being able to walk adds a lot of excitement to his life.
He can explore even more than he could by crawling, no
matter how rapidly he was traveling through your home. He
can move faster, reach higher, and enjoy life even more.

*Heidi has been walking since she was 10 months
old, and she started taking steps at 8 months. You tell
her to come here, and she'll turn around and go the
other way. She's very good at ignoring you. If she's
entering the negative stage, she's getting good at it!*
Jenny

Starting to walk at ten months is unusual. Most children
wait until they're 12 to 14 months old, and some are even

older when they take those first steps. If you're nervous because your 17-month-old son isn't walking yet, talk with your doctor.

Your child will probably cruise from one piece of furniture to another, perhaps for several weeks, before he starts walking on his own. When he finally walks, his balance and coordination won't be well-developed. He'll stretch his arms out to his sides and walk with his legs somewhat spread apart. At first he'll lean slightly forward and take short steps.

Soon his rhythm will improve. Sometime during this stage he'll be able to stoop down, pick something up, and carry it around. Notice how proud he is of this new talent.

Before long he will walk pulling or pushing a toy. This is the time for the corn popper or other push/pull toy. He much prefers a toy that makes a noise as he pulls or pushes it along.

He doesn't need shoes until he starts walking outside. In fact, walking barefoot helps strengthen his feet and arches.

When you buy shoes for him, be sure they fit well, look comfortable, and aren't too big. There should be about one-half inch of space between his big toe and the end of his shoe. You'll have to replace his shoes often because his feet will grow so quickly. As long as they fit well, it's all right to buy the cheapest brand of shoes you can find. Sneakers are fine.

He Jabbers Before He Talks

Marty sits there jabbering. He sounds like he knows what he's talking about, but I can't understand what he's saying.

Yumiko, 16 - Marty, 21 months

Talking means jabbering at this stage. He may say his first word about the time of his first birthday. He will

She's learning to talk, but first she jabbers.

communicate mostly through gestures for awhile yet. He's eager to learn more words, so play the labeling game with him. Point to an object and name it, then wait for him to repeat the name. "Table." "Chair." "Kitty." He may try to say the word after you.

Will your child be bilingual? If two languages are spoken in your home, you probably will want him to learn both. Some people suggest that one parent or caregiver always speak one language to the child, and the other parent or caregiver speak the second language. They feel the child will be able to keep the two languages separate more easily when this happens.

> *My mom talks to Kamie in Spanish a lot. I've been lagging in that, but I do want her to be bilingual.*
>   Lucas, 21 - Kamie, 21 months

If he's learning two languages, his overall language ability may develop a little more slowly than will the language of a child learning only one. By the time he enters kindergarten, he should speak both languages well. If you can teach your child to become bilingual, you're giving him a valuable gift.

She Copies Mom and Dad

Alice likes to try to write, perhaps because I've been writing a lot of letters this year and she likes to watch me.

She tries to put the key in the door like I do.

Melanie

She likes to copy you. She may feed you pieces of her food, then smile broadly if you take it. She probably loves having you copy her. You can copy her movements and her play activities. She's likely to be delighted.

Copying you is one of her best learning techniques. If you stack a block on top of another, she may do the same thing. If you demonstrate drinking from a cup, she may learn a little more quickly. Her speech, of course, depends a great deal on your modeling.

Your toddler may enjoy showing off. Her sense of humor may be developing nicely:

Alice makes faces at me, sniffles her nose, laughs. If she does something people like and they laugh, she grins real big. Lots of times when she does something we like, we clap. Then she starts clapping for herself.

Melanie

Letting her know you like what she's doing is the best way to help her develop a good sense of self-esteem. This won't be hard for you to do because you'll be excited about her achievements.

I praise her to make her feel good. You have to make her feel good so she'll be a good kid.

I wasn't brought up like this. I had a pretty rough childhood. My mom was young, and she wasn't around. She left me with my grandparents, and my grandpa would say, "Oh, you're so stupid."

Miguel, 20 - Genny, 18 months

Emotions Develop Rapidly

Her emotions come through clearly. If there's already a new baby, she probably will be jealous as well as affectionate toward the new sibling:

When Sylvia was first born, Crystal didn't like her too well and would hit her. I let her help with the baby and didn't make her feel she was being thrown out. I explained that Sylvia was her baby, too.

Now if anybody makes Sylvia cry, Crystal will protect her. When her little cousin hits Sylvia, Crystal hits him.

Carrie, 18 - Crystal, 31 months; Sylvia, 14 months

She may be wary of strangers, and even of some people she knows. She doesn't like to be picked up too quickly by people she doesn't know well. She's her own person and doesn't want to be grabbed by adults.

Alice is real open with most people unless they want to pick her up right away. When she gets used to them, she'll go to them.

Melanie

Your Problem-Solving Toddler

Todd is so busy. I wonder how he got all that energy. I'll put little crackers in a container, and give him a second container with it. He'll put the crackers back and forth from one to the other. You can see how

*his little mind works — he'll try to put half on this
side and half on the other.*

*It's unbelievable how much he knows, I guess more
than I really give him credit for.*

Jill, 18 - Todd, 16 months

As Jill said, you can almost see his mind developing.
He's learning more rapidly now than he ever will again.
His world is expanding constantly, and he's trying to keep
up with it.

You might like to research your child's ability to solve a
problem through trial and error. Perhaps she's trying to ride
her kiddy car between two pieces of furniture. She discovers she can't get through, so scoots around the furniture

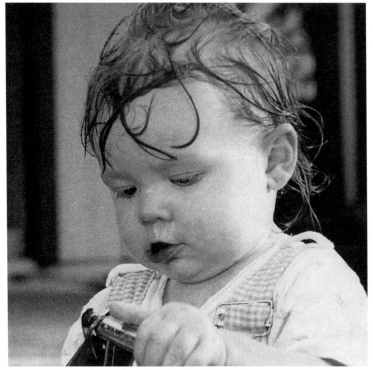

She's trying hard to figure it out.

instead. That's the trial and error method. Something didn't work, so she tried something else.

Tatiana is using the trial and error method to get on the furniture:

We have very tall furniture, tall couches and tall chairs. Tatiana tries to crawl up on them. If she can't, she will go get her own little chair, and use it to stand on to get up on the couch. She likes to sit on the big furniture like we do.

Yesterday she was using her little chair to get on the cabinet, but I told her not to. I think that's a little too dangerous.

Mihaela, 16 - Tatiana, 18 months

From Bottle or Breast to Cup

If you haven't started encouraging your child to drink milk, juice, and water from a cup, it's time to do so. Children generally can begin to learn to drink from a cup when they're about nine months old, sometimes even earlier.

Weaning your child from his bottle or your breast is likely to go more smoothly if he's had plenty of time to learn to drink from a cup. Drinking from a cup is quite different from sucking fluid from a bottle.

The milk enters his mouth faster from a cup, and it comes into the front of his mouth instead of the back. Not only will he not be able to suck, he will need to learn how to hold his lower lip along the edge of the cup. Otherwise, the milk will dribble down his chin.

Many children like to use a cup with a drinking spout. They can still suck a little, and the spout is more like a nipple than is the edge of a cup. Transferring to a cup later won't be especially difficult.

For some children, giving up the bottle is difficult. Some

people believe it's easier for the child (and mom and dad) if he switches from his bottle to a cup soon after he's a year old. They feel if he takes his bottle until he's two, for example, he won't want to change — almost like an addiction.

On the other hand, some children appear to need more sucking than others. They suck a thumb or a pacifier for satisfaction. Your child's need to suck will be less as she nears her second birthday. You're the best judge of your child's readiness to give up her bottle.

I always held him when he was little while he took his bottle. I would think that if I was little, and I saw this big bottle in my mouth, nobody around, nobody paying any attention to me, I know how I would feel. So I would always hold him and talk to him while he had his bottle.

Charity, 17 - Casey, 18 months

As you give your baby a bottle of milk, hold her in your lap while you feed her. A child under two will let you know when she's ready to give up the bottle. She will drink a little, then look away or start to play. Two things need to happen at that time:

She has to get enough milk — or get enough calcium from another source such as yogurt and cottage cheese.

You have to be comfortable that she's telling you she doesn't need the sucking experience any longer.

If your child is hungry at bedtime, give her a light snack or a bottle *before* she goes to bed. Then brush her teeth. If she still needs something to suck on as she drifts off to sleep, give her a bottle of water or a pacifier. Either will satisfy her urge to suck.

There is nothing wrong with going to bed with a bottle of water. That's just fine. It's a nice comforting thing, and

all of us like to be comfortable when we go to bed. But it is
not good, whatever your child's age, to have milk in that
bottle.

If your child goes to sleep with a bottle of milk in his
mouth, the sugar in the milk is likely to cause cavities in his
teeth — the Nursing Bottle Syndrome. If your toddler
wants a bottle at bedtime, put water in the bottle.

*Alice will take two or three naps during the day.
She's attached to her bottle. At night she has to go to
sleep with the bottle, but she doesn't care what's in it.
I give her water at night.*

*If I give her milk in a cup and water in the bottle,
maybe she'll quit demanding the bottle so much.*

Melanie

Helping Baby's Brain Develop

Your baby's brain cells were almost entirely developed
when she was born. The connections baby needs in order to
allow learning occur after birth at an extremely fast rate for
the first few years.

Some parts of his brain will not change much after birth.
But much of the brain is "plastic" — it's shaped by its
surroundings and by repeated experiences. A person's
capacity for abstract learning and thinking is particularly
plastic.

Your child's most rapid brain growth happens in his first
three years. By the time he is 2, in fact, his brain has twice
as many connectors (*synapses*) as an adult's. This early
growth spurt is complete by age 10. Synapses that have not
been stimulated die off.

If you love your baby a lot and respond to her cries for
food, warmth, dryness, cuddling, and sleep, she will probably do well during her first six to eight months. In

addition, it's important to read, sing, talk, and play with your child. Your reading, singing, talking and playing with her will have a major impact on her brain development.

One study showed that only 50 percent of infants and toddlers have parents who read to them regularly. Not reading to one's child means that child is at risk of not learning as she should. She may not become as capable and intelligent as she could have been.

Being "at risk" means the desired behavior/learning will not happen automatically. Much learning at this stage occurs because she is copying your example. Unless you help her, she may not talk as well as she might. Unless you guide her in learning to get along with people, her social development won't be as good as it should be. How you respond to her needs today has a great deal to do with the person she becomes.

Your child is an exciting challenge. Your love and your guidance provide the foundation for her future.

She puts her shoes on now, but sometimes she needs help.

2

She's Struggling for Independence

- **Toddlers, Like Teenagers, Struggle for Independence**
- **When Your Child Asks for Help**
- **"Terrible Twos"**
- **Her Skills Increase Rapidly**
- **Coping with Fears**
- **Don't Rush Toilet Teaching**
- **Major Tasks for Parents**
- **Most Important Stage in Life**

Marty hates the word "No." If I say "No," he wants to do the opposite. He's very active. I say anything, and he picks it up, sometimes in sentences.

He likes clothes. He likes to put his training pants on and off. He likes hats. He likes dolls. He's even starting to learn to swim.

Yumiko, 16 - Marty, 21 months

Kamie says "NO." That was one of her first words. She's very talkative.

She puts on her pants and her socks herself. She knows how to open doors, turn on the TV, change the channel.

She's always alert, wanting to do new things, I
think maybe because we give her so much attention.
When she does things, we clap.
    Sometimes I think, what would she be like if I
weren't here?

Lucas, 21 - Kamie, 21 months

The runabout stage in a child's life is one of the most
difficult for his parents — and for himself. He's trying to
move away from being a dependent baby. So far, he has
relied on other people for almost everything. Now he wants
to be an independent person who makes many of his own
decisions and who is rather self-reliant. To develop prop-
erly, he needs to take this step, hard as it is on those
around him.

Infants are okay, but with toddlers, you have to
kind of know what you're doing. And you have to take
it one day at a time.

Roseanna, 14 - Felipe, 2

Toddlers, Like Teenagers, Struggle for Independence

The toddler's "negative stage" has been compared to the
beginning of puberty. At that time, as you may remember,
young people struggle toward becoming adults who make
their own decisions. No longer does the adolescent want
her parents to "run her life." A great deal of friction occurs
in many families because of the parents' desire to stay in
control of their teenager's life while the teenager insists
on taking over that control. It's often a difficult time
for everyone.

Your toddler probably has similar feelings. No, she
doesn't want the family car tonight, but she does want to
feel she is in control of what she eats, the clothes she wears,

when/whether she uses the bathroom, and how long she plays outside. Giving her the opportunity to make some of these decisions may make it easier for her to comply with your wishes when you can't let her choose.

> *Henry is a handful. He doesn't really mess things up and break things, but he climbs, gets into every-thing. I'm constantly having to watch him while I'm doing everything else. It gets very hectic.*
>
> *Every time I tell him to do something, he says "No." Sometimes I put him in the bedroom and shut the door. He'll bang on the door and cry, and that gets on my nerves. When I get really uptight, I let Marvin take care of him, and I get out of the house.*
>
> Olivia, 21 - Henry, 23 months

Teenagers and their parents are ahead if they can each give a little. Perhaps she can't have the family car when-ever she wants it, but she can use it for errands and an occasional evening out with friends. Perhaps she can't stay out as late as she chooses, but maybe she and her parents can arrive at a reasonable compromise.

The consequences of treating adolescents either too strictly or too loosely may be severe. They still need paren-tal support, but they also need to be able to take responsi-bility for their own actions. Teenagers who either lose control of themselves or have never learned to take control of their lives can end up with serious difficulties. They not only may have trouble with other people, but with the law as well.

Parents and toddlers, too, need to adjust to each others' wishes. Your toddler needs to feel she has some control over her life just as you do. A major difference between a teen's struggle for independence and a toddler's struggle is that your toddler can't yet express herself well using words.

How would you feel if you had faced the difficulties of adolescence without being able to talk very well? You'd probably feel terribly frustrated.

Compromise and respect are magic ingredients for minimizing the frustrations of living with a toddler. Being sensitive to your child's need to control some aspects of her life will help you understand her behavior better.

When Your Child Asks for Help

As your child becomes more and more independent, she will get upset if she can't do what she wants to do. Yet, her language has not developed enough to tell you what she's feeling and what she wants. She's frustrated, and she can't explain what's wrong because she doesn't know the words. The result may be a tantrum.

Responding when your child asks for help is the best way to cut down on the number of tantrums she will have:

- When your child wants you, stop to see what she wants.
- Provide the help she needs if possible.
- Talk briefly at your child's level of understanding about the event.
- Once you have assisted or comforted and talked to your child, your next step is to leave her alone.

Because of your sensitivity to her needs, your child learns a lot from an interchange like this:

- She learns to use another person (you) as a resource when she can't handle a situation herself.
- She learns that someone thinks her discomfort, excitement, or problem is important, which means she is important.
- Her language skills also get a boost each time this happens.

For more suggestions on helping your child deal with a temper tantrum, see *Discipline from Birth to Three* by Lindsay and McCullough.

"Terrible Twos"

This is Kaylie's "NO" stage. I figure she's at the age where she'll say "No" regardless of what I tell her. Right now, she's mostly running around, screaming and yelling, having fun.

Samantha, 16 - Kaylie, 20 months

Often, people speak of the "Terrible Twos" as if extreme negative behavior suddenly turns up after a child's second birthday. For some children, however, this negative attitude starts as early as 13 or 14 months.

At least by the time he is 17 months old, your child will probably enter this difficult phase. He will often want his own way, no matter what. No longer can you distract him by offering a substitute for the forbidden activity. If he sees that you disapprove of whatever he's doing, he may be even more determined to continue doing it. He will often be hard to live with.

Two thoughts may comfort you. First, this happens to just about every child. His negative actions certainly do not mean you are a poor parent or a terrible person, nor does it mean your child is a brat. Second, his extreme negative behavior will probably go away, or at least become much less intense, within a few months. Perhaps by his second birthday, you will find living with him is a little easier.

For many of us, becoming independent is a real struggle from birth to adulthood. When your toddler seems extra difficult, remember that being a toddler is even harder than caring for one. Your toddler needs all the help and respect you can provide.

If Marty doesn't know how to put something to-
gether, he'll get help. If he wants to read a book, he
brings it to me. He pulls the legs off his plastic doll
and brings them to me. He's pretty independent.
Sometimes if I walk up and try to help him, he seems
to be saying, "Mom, I can do it, leave me alone."

Yumiko

You still need to be firm about things that matter, but
give him choices whenever possible. Don't say, "Come to
lunch right this minute." Instead, a few minutes before
lunch is ready, ask, "Do you want to wash your hands for
lunch, or shall I help you?" At bedtime you might say,
"Which book do you want me to read tonight?" During this
negative stage, don't ever say, "Do you want lunch?" or
"Do you want to go to bed?" unless you can handle "No"
for your answer.

Avoid showing your power when possible. Don't order
him to do something unless it's really necessary. If it is
necessary, then of course you insist that he go along with
your wishes.

Routines and a regular schedule, not only for bedtime,
but also for meals, naps, baths, and dressing, may help. Let
him do it himself as much as possible. At times, he will
insist on doing it himself when you know he can't possibly
succeed. He may get terribly frustrated, but still won't let
you help him.

You need far more tact in dealing with a toddler than
with the most temperamental spouse or employer in exist-
ence. Remember — being tactful is simply being sensitive
to another person's feelings.

How much should you help your child? He needs to
continue to be able to call on you as his resource for help
when he needs it. Sometimes a child of this age seems not
to want to work things out for himself. If he always wants

mother to help him put the puzzle together, either it's too hard for him, or he isn't learning to be as independent as he should be.

Use your best judgment. Help him when you think he needs you — if he wants you to or will let you. Guide him toward more independence when you think this is advisable.

Her Skills Increase Rapidly

By your child's second birthday, she may be able to pedal a small tricycle. If she has had practice, she can walk down stairs alone, but she still needs to hang on to the stair railing.

Your almost-two-year-old may be running more than she walks. She can walk on low walls if you hold one of her hands. She can even walk a few steps on tiptoe if you show her how.

By this age, she can take off her clothes, and even put most of them back on. It helps if you choose easy-to-put-on clothing. In fact, when you're shopping for her and looking at items, consider the ease with which she can help dress herself. Easy-to-put-on clothes can save her — and you — a lot of frustration.

If you choose clothes with big buttons or zippers and shoes with Velcro fasteners, you'll make it easier for her. Wide sleeves with big armholes and wide-necked garments will also help.

Coping with Fears

If your child is afraid of the noise of trains and trucks, toilet flushing, police sirens, or the vacuum cleaner, be patient with her.

She may have other fears. Whatever they are, they are real to her. Telling her it's "nothing to be afraid of" won't make it better. Accept the fears as the real feelings they are.

Gently help her cope. If she's afraid of the dark, for example, provide a little night light. If she's fearful of storms, let her stay close to you until it's over. If you're not afraid, she probably will follow your example eventually.

Don't Rush Toilet Teaching

Toilet teaching (training) is not an appropriate task for most children under two. Their brains and bodies have not matured enough yet. They simply are not ready. Efforts spent at toilet teaching a child too soon result mostly in frustration for parents and child.

For a discussion of toilet teaching, see *Discipline from Birth to Three* by Lindsay and McCullough.

Major Tasks for Parents

As a parent of a child just learning to get around, you have three major tasks. First, you need to design your child's world so that she can satisfy her curiosity without getting hurt and without causing damage to your home. If you can child-proof your house or apartment and your yard, you'll be doing your child and yourself a favor.

Your second job is to react to your child when she wants you. She may want your help because she's frustrated at something she can't do herself. She may have hurt herself slightly and needs comforting. Or she may be excited and want you to share her excitement. Your assistance, comfort, and enthusiasm are important to her.

It's crucial to your child's learning that you respond promptly to her needs and to her interests. If you're talking on the phone, it's better to say, "I'm talking on the phone. I'll be with you in a minute," than it is to ignore her. Of course, you'll then need to be with her "in a minute."

Your third major responsibility with your child is to

carry out your role as authority. Being firm is often necessary. Don't say "No" constantly, or you'll destroy some of your child's curiosity. When you do say "No," mean what you say.

If you say "No," then laugh because she looks pretty funny sitting in the middle of the dining table playing in the sugar bowl, will she take you seriously? Instead, say "No," get her down from the table, and put the sugar bowl away.

The important thing is to see that she carries out your requests. At this age, this generally means removing your child from the situation or distracting her. Ideally, you won't say "No" a second time because you'll already have taken care of the problem.

Most Important Stage in Life

Marty explores everything. He opens doors, closets, drawers, pulls all his clothes out. I just go in there and pick them up and make him help. It's not that drastic when a kid pulls his clothes out of his drawer. When he's old enough, he'll fold them up himself. Now he helps . . . he hands them to me.

Yumiko

Helping your toddler develop well is perhaps the greatest challenge you will ever face. How she develops socially and intellectually now is the basis for all of her future development in these areas. Her growth in language and curiosity during this time is of vital importance.

While parenting during this stage has many difficult times, you will also find lots of enjoyment in a well developing toddler. You will find you're no longer living with a baby but, rather, with a young and very interesting little person.

Enjoy your child!

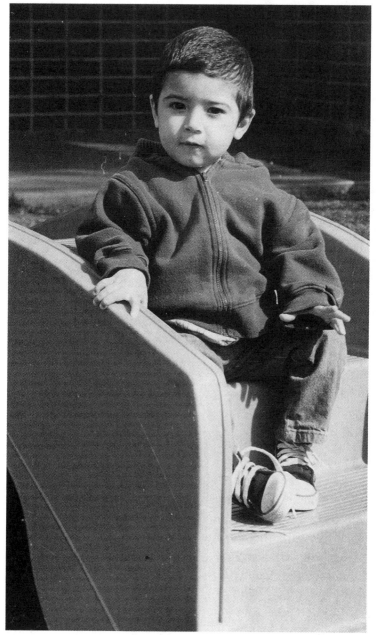

He likes to practice climbing the steps.

3

Active Play — A Toddler's Work

- Play *with* Your Child
- Active Play Is Valuable
- Play Ball!
- Play Space, Play Time Needed
- Play with Him Often
- Classifying Objects
- Plan for Indoor Play
- Making Toys at Home

What I like about her is she's fun. She's real playful with almost everybody. You play with her just a little bit and she'll smile a lot. She always has a smile on her face. People say she looks like me. I like taking her with me to the park when I go there with my friends to play handball.

Marcus, 16 - Liliane, 15 months

Meghan likes to figure things out. She loves things that are not toys, especially her father's tools and hammers. Of course she only plays with them when daddy is right beside her.

She loves to play with keys, to

unlock the doors like mommy and daddy. She likes to play outside with the kids, but she still comes in often to check on me.

When I take her to the park, she climbs. At first, she wanted me to come get her down from each thing, but I thought she should learn a little independence. I would sort of close my eyes and not help her for awhile. It seemed mean, but I thought if I'm there to do it, she'll expect Mommy to help her all the time.

Louise, 19 - Meghan, 22 months; Mark, 5 months

Play *with* Your Child

Playing with your child is important. He loves to play with you. As you play, stop occasionally to watch him without interrupting his play. You can learn a lot about the ways he likes to play. Let him lead you into playing at his level.

Building elaborate block structures while he watches is not exactly playing *with* him. He won't learn as much if he simply watches you as he will if he's actively playing.

During this time he will start holding things in both hands. He'll stack blocks on top of each other. Emptying and filling containers may keep him entertained for a considerable time.

As his language develops, ask him to talk about his play. What is he doing? If he's scribbling or coloring, ask him about his picture. Don't say, "What is that?" Instead, suggest, "Tell me about your drawing." Remember that his attention span is still very short. When he decides to stop playing, respect his judgment.

Active Play Is Valuable

Trilby just started walking, and she's doing real good. She's real playful, always wanting to play.

*I take her to the park and we play around. We put
her in the baby swing, and she loves it. I sing to her. I
do everything I can.*

Saunders, 17 - Trilby, 13 months

Running, climbing, jumping, swinging, and generally
leaping about are all important for your toddler's development. Playground equipment can be exciting for her if it's
not too large or elaborate and hard to use. If she can climb
it herself, and if she wants to, she's probably safe, and will
be able to get down by herself.

If you help her get up on the equipment, you may have
to help her get down. Let her do as much as she can by
herself. Don't help her much, and don't urge her to play on
something about which she feels fearful. Sometimes you
may need to help her get down or simply remove her from
equipment that is too dangerous.

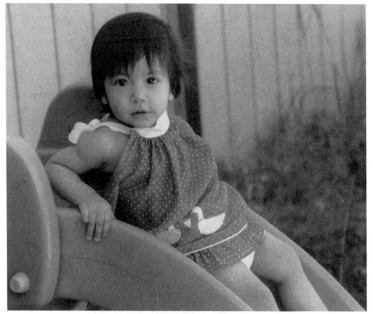

This slide is just her size.

Toddlers generally love to swing. Do you have a tree or something else to use for hanging a swing? An old tire on a strong rope makes a great swing. Some toddlers would rather be pushed in the swing than do almost anything else.

If you have your own house, you might put a couple of strong hooks in the joists or rafters above a play space. Securely tie a thick soft rope to the hooks. Put a big knot at the other end. Your child can hold on to it and try to straddle it. Later, when she's older, you might even put a rope ladder on it for her. This could be a good project for grandpa.

Acrobatics are fun for toddlers. Is there any way you can let her play on an old crib mattress on the floor? Jumping on your bed can be pretty destructive and dangerous if she should fall off. If you have an old mattress or foam rubber pad you can put on the floor, she'll love playing on it.

Shelly is very active. She'll watch people do something, then try to copy them. My cousin does gymnastics, and she tries to do what he does.
                                      Dixie, 18 - Shelly, 17 months

If you don't have stairs in your home, find some occasionally so she can practice going up and down. Otherwise, with no practice in coming down safely, she's apt to fall when she's at the top of a flight of stairs.

Shelly is good at stairs now. She used to fall. She climbs them on her knees, then comes down on her butt. At first, it was a problem. When she was real quiet, I'd know she was going upstairs. I let her go, but I was right behind her.
                                      Dixie

A board about eight inches wide and six feet long makes a good "toy." Your toddler can use it for a balancing board.

Putting one foot directly in front of the other is a hard task for toddlers. She can practice on the board. She can also practice this skill on the lines of your floor tiles.

Walking the plank is even more fun if you set it up on two low piles of magazines. An inch above the floor is plenty high at first. Later, your child will be able to walk up when one end is raised slightly.

She'll enjoy riding toys although she may not be ready for a tricycle until she's at least two. Best is a low kiddy car in which she can sit and push herself along with her feet. You need to look for one that is simply built and won't spread her legs too far apart. Remember that toddlers have short legs. Some plastic cars are built too wide.

Competent as your toddler is, you still need *always* to supervise water play, whether in the bathtub or outdoors. She will continue to enjoy this kind of play, especially if you join her. She may even be able to blow soap bubbles very soon.

Remember, however, that a child can drown in an inch of water. She should *never* be left alone with even a little water in the tub or play pool.

Play Ball!

We play ball. I throw the ball, the dog picks it up, and brings it to me, puts it down. Todd then picks it up and throws it.

We always play chase in the house. I act like I'm a monster and I'm going to get him. He loves it.

Jill, 18 - Todd, 16 months

Sean throws a big ball and kicks it. He's been playing with it for about two weeks. He has a smaller one that he throws around and kicks, too.

Ginger, 18 - Sean, 17 months

Sometime after her first birthday, she will enjoy simple ball games. By the time she's two, she may be able to throw overhand more or less in your direction. She can kick a ball, too.

A tennis ball can provide a lot of fun for a toddler. She can have a wonderful time throwing it and watching it bounce. It's easier for her to handle than is a bigger ball. Perhaps best of all, she's less likely to knock a lamp over, put out a window, or hurt another child with a tennis ball.

She picks up everything. She tries to play baseball. She'll hit it and do the running. She always slides into base. She's a real character.

Darla, 17 - Janis, 2

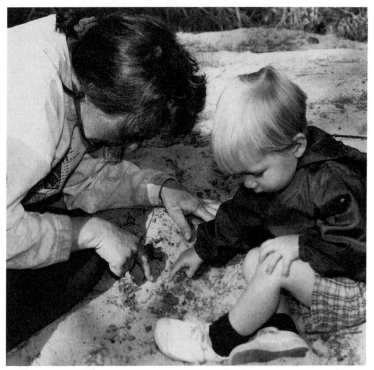

He and Mom have a good time exploring together.

Play Space, Play Time Needed

Tatiana likes toys that make a lot of noise, that ring, that talk to her. She likes the telephone more than anything. We have this phone where we can push the button and it sounds like it's ringing. We tell her to answer the phone. When I'm talking to someone, she thinks I'm talking to her, and she answers back on her phone.

She has a little plastic slide in her room. She likes to play on it, but not as much as she likes going outside.

Mihaela, 16 - Tatiana, 18 months

Wherever you live, even if it's a crowded apartment, try to make play space for your toddler. It's still best if this space can be part of the kitchen or living room close to you rather than in a room away from everyone.

Organizing your child's play materials is important. If he can't find part of the toy he wants, he won't play as well. Does he seem to have lots of toys that he doesn't use? Are some of them broken? Are there parts missing? Are they hard to find at the bottom of a deep toy box? Are they hidden behind storage doors?

Perhaps you can get a few open shelves. Concrete blocks and boards, if not stacked too high, make good shelving. Make sure they are stable so your toddler can't push them down. Help him keep his big toys on the bottom shelf, his others where he can reach them.

It's wise to have only a few toys readily available, the toys he's really interested in at the time. When you bring his other toys out again, they may seem new and interesting. If you leave everything out, a child this age will simply throw them all over the floor. You may even want him to use the more complicated stacking toys only at times when you can play with him.

Roseanna, 14, and Felipe, 2, lived in a small apartment with little storage space. Roseanna placed several hooks high on the wall. On each hook she hung a pillowcase of toys. They came down for play one at a time.

The apartment was less of a disaster area, and Felipe's play undoubtedly was more satisfying to him. He wasn't confused by seeing all his toys dumped out at once.

Mihaela mentioned a similar tactic. She switches toys daily for Tatiana, keeping some in the closet and putting others out for her use.

Play With Him Often

Jamaica likes to read books. She likes puzzles and blocks, and loves her dolls.

She likes to get in the tub with me. She loves to play in the water. Just being around each other makes us more happy.

Kyli, 17 - Jamaica, 22 months

I love this age when Derek is running around. It makes me feel good that I can teach him something.

After dinner he starts winding up again, so I usually take him for a walk. He wants to know what everything is. By the time we get back, he's pretty calm again.

Laurette, 17 - Derek, 18 months

Laurette is a wise mother. Taking Derek for a walk when he's "wound up" is much better for both of them, far better than his mother insisting he "Calm down right now!" In addition, chances are good that Derek will be ready for bed after he's had his walk with his mom.

Play with your child regularly. Hopefully, you'll do this because you want to. Of course your work and activities take a lot of time, and they — and you — are very important. But if he has to whine and beg to get your attention, the ten minutes of play you finally give him won't be much fun for either of you.

> *I just bought Jayme a big fire truck, and he likes to run that around. Or we play with Disney pop-up toys. He likes to go with my brother and pretend he's playing Nintendo with him.*
> *We go for walks. We play at the park.*
> Kaylene, 18 - Jayme, 16 months

Make the most of whatever time you can give your child. Be sure to give him your full attention. Follow his lead. Does he want to roll a ball back and forth? Then play ball with him.

Tomorrow he may decide to let you help him build a tower with his blocks, or perhaps he'll be ready to finger paint. Always talk to him about whatever you're doing together.

A follow-the-leader game is easy to organize right in your living room. You be the leader first. You might crawl under the table, around a chair, through a big box you've placed there, and over the big ball beside the box. Next time, let your child be the leader.

Bowling Game
Use half-gallon milk cartons for bowling pins. You may need to put blocks or sand inside them to give them enough stability to stand up. Then show your child how to roll a ball toward the "pins" to try to knock them over.

Throwing newspaper balls is fun for a toddler and remarkably safe for your house. Crumple newspaper into a ball and hold it together with a little tape. Make several and offer them to your child.

If he's naming small objects such as a ball, a car, a spoon, and a doll, make him a feel-box. A box in which small appliances are shipped is usually sturdy enough for this game. Cut a hole in the side big enough for your child's hand.

Show him the little items one at a time. Let him handle and examine them. Then put each one inside the box. Ask him to put his hand in the box and pick up an item. Then, without taking it out or looking at it, ask him to tell you what it is.

Classifying Objects

You may notice your toddler is beginning to sort items into groups. This is a start toward making sense out of his world by classifying things and people into categories. He has already classified people into those he knows and trusts and those he doesn't. He certainly classifies toys into "mine" and, more slowly, "yours."

When you purchase toys for him, a good set of small objects is a good buy. Be sure none of the parts are so small that he could choke on them. Perhaps you'll choose a city street scene or a barn with animals and people. You'll find he begins playing by classifying — dividing the people from the animals, for example. Soon he will be creating scenes and using his imagination. He'll make the cars go fast, the dogs chase one another, and the policemen stop traffic.

Another "game" idea — suggest she sort the laundry or her clothes by color.

Plan for Indoor Play

Casey is very busy now, into everything. He's happy — he thinks he's the funniest person in the world, and I agree with him!

He's starting to learn movements to songs. He dances, and I dance with him. I turn on the radio and dance with him.

He's learning a lot right now. He's learning new words. I sing the alphabet to him.

Charity, 17 - Casey, 18 months

Painting outside means less mess inside.

Scribbling has been called the art of the toddler. Scribbling is how she learns to draw. Instead of teaching her to draw later, show her how to scribble during her second year. Her scribbling will turn into drawing a year or so from now.

Putting out big sheets of paper for painting and scribbling is important. You don't have to buy paper. Just put in front of your child big paper bags that have been cut open. First, you put a mark on the paper with an oversized kindergarten crayon. Then hand the crayon to her saying, "Now you color." She will love it. She will also need supervision

unless you want the scribbling extended to your walls,
furniture, and telephone book. For more about this, see
Discipline from Birth to Three.

It's time to make or buy a few simple puzzles for your
child. Paste a picture on cardboard, then cut it in three
pieces. Can she fit them together? If she does it quickly,
perhaps she's ready for a harder task. If so, cut the same
puzzle into five or six pieces. Can she still put it together?

She can probably place a circle and a square in a
formboard. You can make one for her by drawing a big
square and circle on a piece of cardboard. Cut out the same
size square and circle from white paper. Color the shapes to
match those on the cardboard. Can she match them yet?

Making Toys at Home

You can make a stacking toy for your child using empty
food containers. Use various sizes of cans such as juice,
tomato paste, and soup cans. Be sure to go around each can
a second time with a can opener. Then feel each one to see
if any sharp edges remain. If it's still sharp, throw it away
and try another can.

Your child will like the designs on the cans, but if you
want something fancier, cover them with glued-on fabric.
Putting fur on one, silk on another, and vinyl on the third
adds nice touching experience to the stacking game.

She may be able to string large "beads" now. The beads
can be empty spools, empty tape rollers, or even hair
rollers. Dip about two inches of the end of some cord in
white glue. Let it dry, and it will be stiff enough for your
toddler to stick it through the holes. The cord should be no
longer than ten inches. You don't want to run the risk of
her wrapping the cord around her neck.

A few months ago, your child probably learned to stack
one block on top of another. Now she can make a higher

stack, a tower of blocks. Or she may stack cans of food, one on top of the other.

Lance climbs right into the cupboards with the pots and pans. Then he puts them inside each other. He can play in the lower cupboards although I rubber-banded one that I don't want him into.

> Celia, 20 - Laurel, 4; Lance, 18 months

She will enjoy rearranging all kinds of objects around the house. She may take everything out of your kitchen cupboard and line the items up on the floor. She may balk at putting them away. If the job seems too much for her, ask her to help you put them back. Perhaps she'd like to sort them by color or size. Then you'd say, "Let's put all the big ones away first." Or make a game of seeing if she can put them away as fast as you put lunch on the table.

Sean explores a lot. He gets into cupboards, every-thing you let him get into. He gets out the pans and bangs them together. He also bangs the cupboard doors back and forth.

> Ginger

Play is your child's work. Through play, she learns more about her world. Joining in her play is an important part of building a good relationship with her. Time spent playing with her is likely to mean less time spent solving problems she causes because of boredom or lack of attention.

Most important, you and your toddler can enjoy each other tremendously!

She has a marvelous time pretending.

4

Her Imagination Soars

- **She Loves to Pretend**
- **Let Him "Help"**
- **Toddlers and Talking**
- **Don't Correct His Speech**
- **Read to Your Child**
- **Choose Non-Sexist Books**
- **You're the Teacher**

Leah talks to her baby dolls. Before we sit down for dinner, she will bring a doll and say, "Baby wants a drink." We catch her whispering to her baby like they're talking to each other.

She mimics me and she repeats a lot of what we say. The other day Leah's mom hurt her arm. Five minutes later Leah came up to me and said, "My arm hurts."

Lyle, 19 - Leah, 2 1/2

Leon pretends he's a dog, a cat, a bird flying. Sometimes he rides a horse (on the arm of the couch). He and DeeDee will go in the bedroom and pretend they're in

outer space. They will sit and talk and talk. He under-
stands her and she understands him.

Tamara, 21 - DeeDee, 41/2; Leon, 20 months

She Loves to Pretend

*Janis does a lot of acting. I got sample diapers in
the mail the other day. She went in and got them and
said, "These are for me. The mailman sent them for
me." She asked me to put them on her, so I did. Then
she pretended she was a baby and crawled around.*

*She likes music a lot, punk rock. She sees my
brother pretend like he's playing a guitar, so she does
it, too.*

Darla, 17 - Janis, 2

Often children in this age group have a marvelous time
pretending. They love to dress up in mother's or daddy's
clothes. Putting on your shoes may be a favorite activity for
him. Different kinds of hats will fascinate him. Save some
of your old clothes for his dress-up play.

*Antonio plays house with his cowboys, soldiers,
and boats. He loves motorcycles — the little ones and
the real ones. We went by the shop yesterday, and he
wanted to get on one.*

*He will tell his doll "No" which is what I tell him.
Or he'll say, "Behave yourself."*

Becky, 18 - Antonio, 26 months

Soon your child may involve you in her make-believe
play. If she invites you to feed her teddy bear, do so. Your
participation is good for her, and besides, you'll have
fun, too.

Dolls are important to almost all children. Most parents
now seem to understand boys need dolls as much as girls

do. After all, if playing with dolls is early practice toward being a parent, it must be as important for boys as for girls. Most men, as well as most women, will become parents.

Janet has two dolls, a boy doll and a bear doll, Frankie and Henry. She takes them in the tub with her. She calls them her babies and takes them to bed.
Candi, 16 - Janet, 18 months

Most toddlers love music. Music stimulates brain development because the child hears it, moves with it, and may sing with it. She may turn the radio on so she'll have music for her dancing. Dance with her if she asks you. You'll both enjoy it. She'd like her own musical instrument such as a drum, cymbals, or musical triangle. You can make her a drum from a one-pound coffee can. Two pan lids make cymbals.

Toddlers love bells. You have to supervise two or more toddlers ringing bells because in their exuberance they might hit each other. It's worth the effort, however.

Let Him "Help"

Henry will open the drawer and get a can opener. Then he'll get a can and give it to me,

Today she's a musician.

or he'll try to open the can himself. He likes to do what I do. He can even unlock the front door himself. We have to watch him constantly.

Olivia, 20 - Henry, 23 months

Toddlers generally love to "help" with the housework. If he can have a small broom, he'll sweep right along with you. Mopping the floor with a rag is his idea of real play.

When you're cooking, you can think of ways to involve him. Let him add the seasonings, pre-measured by you, of course. If you're baking, he can sift ingredients and help you stir the mixture.

If you can figure a way to let him help you wash dishes without having a nervous breakdown yourself, he'll love it. If you have two sinks, he can use one to wash plastic spoons, cups, plates, and pans. You'll probably be ahead if you put a lot of newspapers on the floor before he starts washing dishes. Then his spills can be rolled up and thrown away. Or put bath towels on the floor to catch the water.

He can be a real help at times. He can follow your simple request, "Bring me the dustcloth." He can help you make the beds, especially his own. He will love to mimic you.

Toddlers and Talking

You've been helping your child learn to speak ever since she was born. You've talked to her, named things and people, read to her. She may be saying quite a few words now.

Sean knows his body parts —nose, eyes, mouth, ears, hands, feet, legs. He just learned his arms yesterday. He answers the telephone. He says, "Who's this?" and then keeps talking.

Ginger, 18 - Sean, 17 months

If there are words you don't want your toddler to learn, try not to have those words said when she's around. She's learning to talk by repeating the words she hears. Punishing a child for using "bad" words doesn't make much sense. To the child, all the words she hears are interesting, and she should not be expected to censor her own speech for several years.

An infant center teacher talked about a two-year-old whose language was outrageous. "We didn't make a big deal of it," she reported. "We ignored the word. We went on as if he didn't say it. We would distract him to something else. Sometimes we'd comment in a matter-of-fact way, 'Oh, we don't use that word.' Then we'd go on to another activity. Gradually his language improved."

Don't Correct His Speech

Now that he's beginning to say a few words, there are two more ways you can help him.

He's saying a few words. Soon he'll be talking.

First, don't correct his speech. When you talk to him, pronounce the words correctly and clearly. But if he says "pitty" for "pretty," don't worry about it. He'll learn faster if you don't criticize.

Second, your child may not bother talking if he sees no need to do so. If he points at the refrigerator, do you immediately hand him a cup of juice? If he gestures for a cracker, do you give it to him right now? Instead, try encouraging him to say the word when possible. Don't frustrate him, of course, by waiting more than a few seconds. Remember that children start talking at different ages.

Shelly pulls at me to get attention. She says "Bottle" and "Eat." If she wants something, she calls it out. She's been doing that for about two months.

Dixie, 18 - Shelly, 17 months

Jayme says "Mommy," "Daddy," "No," "Yes," "grandma," and especially, "What's this?" He's pretty curious about everything.

He responds when I talk with him. We can actually carry on a conversation.

Kaylene, 18 - Jayme, 16 months

While most children can name familiar things and occasionally speak in two-word phrases toward the end of the second year, your perfectly bright two-year-old may say scarcely a word. Don't worry about it. Continue talking to him about the things you're doing with him. Use simple, clear, slow speech. By the end of this stage, your child may be talking in "sentences." His version of a sentence, however, is generally one word such as "Hi." If he says "Up," he means "Pick me up." Don't expect sentences complete with a noun, a verb, and an object. Most children don't speak in real sentences until after their second birthday.

> ## Book of (his name)'s Words
> Use light cardboard for the pages. The cardboard in
> panty hose packages works well. Punch holes in the
> pages and tie them together with yarn. Find pictures to
> represent the words he's saying. "Ma-ma," "Da-da,"
> "Bye," and "Dog" may be his first understandable words.
> Put a picture of each in the book, then read it with him.
> Soon he may be "reading" the pictures to you.

Read to Your Child

If you've been reading to your child, he's probably
talking more than he would have otherwise.

*I read to Shelly. I think that helps her learn to
talk. I started reading to her when she was ten
months old.*

*I don't like to read unless it's what I want to read.
But when I read to Shelly, I know what I'm getting out
of it. I enjoy it. And she starts mumbling as though
she's reading. That's how she learned the name
doggie, etc. She turns the pages herself.*

Dixie

*Sean takes a book, opens it up, and jabbers like
he's reading. I read to him a lot. He likes to point at
the pictures, and he listens when I read to him.*

Ginger

The pictures are the important thing. Don't get hung up
on teaching your child to read for several years yet. You
can count on him learning to read with less struggle later if
he enjoys books with you now. When you choose books for
your toddler, you'll want those with bright, simple pictures.
At this age, her favorites will probably be books with
pictures of things and people she already knows about.

*Heidi loves picture books. I read to her. She has
books in her toy box. She looks at them, then shows
me and grunts that she wants me to read to her. It's
really amazing how she wants to talk so bad.*

Jenny, 18 - Heidi, 13 months

If her grandparents live with or near you, a book about a
child playing with Gramps will interest her. Books about
dogs and cats are good. She may especially like stories
with pictures of babies.

As she grows older, of course, you won't limit her
books to stories about familiar things. The rhythm of
Mother Goose
rhymes will appeal
to her. Fairy tales
and stories about
animals, people,
and places she has
never seen are an
important part of
her education.
Provide lots of
variety in her
books, because
books can widen
her knowledge of
and interest in
many different
things. Books
about familiar
topics, however,
are more likely to
keep a toddler's
interest.

Reading with Mom is a special time.

Choose Non-Sexist Books

Books can play an important part in a child's learning about himself and his world. Don't let his books show a slanted, sexist picture of the world. Too often, children's picture books portray most mothers in the kitchen cooking dinner and fathers out earning the living.

Children's picture books sometimes suggest through illustrations and words that little girls stay clean, play quietly, and cry occasionally. Little boys, however, are expected to play roughly and get dirty, but aren't supposed to cry.

Look for books that show boys and girls, men and women, as human beings with lots of different abilities and interests. Don't choose stories and illustrations that suggest that your child must limit his/her interests because of his/her sex.

You want your daughter to be glad she's a girl. You want your son to be glad he's a boy. But an athlete, a doctor, or a police officer can be glad she's a woman. A nurse, a dancer, or a preschool teacher can be glad he's a man. Books can help your child realize the wonderful opportunities open to boys and girls, to men and to women. Choose those books carefully.

You're the Teacher

As you read to your child and encourage the development of his imagination, you're laying the foundation for reading and other successful school experiences for him later. In fact, you are your child's most important teacher. He will learn far more interacting with you during this stage than he ever will again.

You have a wonderful challenge!

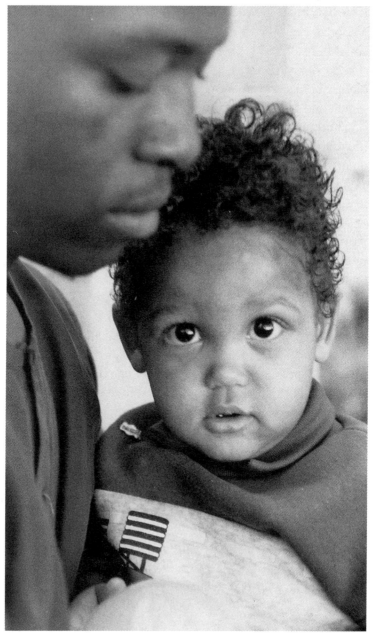

Both Dad and toddler win if Dad's involved.

5

Dad's Ahead
If He's Involved

- **Some Fathers Are Very Involved**
- **Others Leave It Up to Mom**
- **Building a Family**
- **Learning to Be a Father**
- **When Dad Lives Elsewhere**
- **Maintaining a Relationship**
- **Your Child Changes Your Life**

I didn't plan it. I didn't expect the pregnancy. We decided to live together after Kamie was born. I want to be in her life because my dad wasn't there for me. I want to see the little things she does. I want to help her, guide her. She's my daughter and I love her.

Parenting is one of the hardest things I've ever experienced. She wakes you up, "I'm hungry, change me, dress me." She loves attention. There are other things I want to do that I can't. It's hard. I do everything. I change her, I feed her, I bathe her. I want to do everything.

Lucas, 21 - Kamie, 21 months

A lot of fathers don't live with their kid. They just come in and visit on weekends or after school, while I can see Alex all the time. I saw him when he started walking, and when he first said "Daddy." That makes me more involved with him.

Alex made me less selfish in a way that I just can't go out and get everything for me. I have to consider that he needs this, he gets that.

I have a lot to share with him. Like now I'm trying to teach him to catch a ball. I'm like every other father in wanting him to be a baseball star, and I want to get him out there young.

I didn't expect to have a baby this young. I hadn't planned on it until I was 25 when I would be stable and set and it was time to have kids. It just happened.

Brian, 20 - Alex, 12 months

Some Fathers Are Very Involved

Teen mothers or fathers who parent alone often have to learn how to take complete responsibility for caring for their child(ren). More often it's the teen mother who cares for the child if the parents aren't together. No matter how tired she is, she's the one who feeds him, plays with him, takes care of him when he's sick, and performs all the other parenting tasks because she's the live-in parent.

Ideally, if the parents live together, they share child care responsibilities. More and more fathers are realizing how much better their relationship with their child is if they're deeply involved in caring for that child. They know that if only mom takes care of the baby, dad misses out:

I'm as involved in Dustin's life as Kelly Ellen is. We both share everything with him. I've felt real attached since the moment he was born.

We both read to him. Books are his favorite now.
Everywhere we go he's got to have books. He has his
favorites.

In sports, you learn everything you can to be the
best you can be. I feel that way about him. I want him
to be brought up the best way we can. Every day is a
different day with him. Every day we learn something,
whether it's his personality change or something we
learn from another child in another family.

I take care of Dustin because I love him. If I didn't
love him, I wouldn't be here. He's part of me, and I
want to be with him and bring him up.

Mark, 22 - Dustin, 21/2 months

Sometimes dad is not the child's biological father. If
mom is with someone else, someone who plays the father
role, she may already know the "real" dad is the one who
loves the child and takes daily responsibility for him.

However, it's always best to be honest with your toddler.
Even if she never sees her biological father, she needs to
know she has another dad. If your partner is not your
child's father, how involved should he be in child care?
That depends on a lot of things. If you're developing a
strong relationship and you expect to be together for a long
time, he will probably want to be quite involved with
your child.

Leesha's real close to Greg. Even though he isn't
her natural father, he's her father. Like when I was
pregnant with Manuel, he would get up in the middle
of the night when Leesha needed him. He's the one
who picks her up from school. That's a father, some-
one who is there for her, who feeds her and bathes
her, not someone who made her.

Kambria, 21 - Leesha, 5; Manuel, 14 months

Others Leave It Up to Mom

Dads do indeed play an important role in a child's life.
Some fathers, however, even if they live with their
children, leave the child care up to mom.

> *Dennis isn't too much help, perhaps because of the
> problems we've had. He thinks the baby is just mine.
> His mom helps me a lot, and my mom did when I lived
> at home. You can get very irritable if you don't have
> anybody to help you.*
>
> Jenny, 18 - Heidi, 13 months

Louise expressed that irritability forcefully:

> *Bob isn't always here, and when he is, he isn't that
> much help. Last night I blew up at him. When he gets
> home, I like to sit down and relax. So I went next door
> to visit a friend.*
>
> *As soon as one of the kids says "Boo," he comes
> over and gets me. I asked him, "Can't I ever leave
> this house to take a break without having you coming
> after me, or Meghan tagging along?"*
>
> *If he goes out that door to visit some of the guys in
> the complex here, I'm not to bother him. It seems like
> mother is supposed to do everything with the kids.*
>
> Louise, 19 - Mark, 5 months; Meghan, 23 months

Mick didn't expect to change his daughter's diapers and
feed her, perhaps because he didn't live with her until she
was 14 months old. In fact, Kris continued doing these
tasks for several months after they moved in with Mick and
his family. Then Kris got a weekend job, and Mick
discovered he had no choice:

> *When Kris and Cassandra moved in with us, I
> didn't think I'd be taking care of Cassie. Then Kris*

started working weekends, so I have Cassie all day Saturday and Sunday. At first I'd say, "Mom, change her."

She would say, "No, you do it."

Or I'd tell my sisters to change her.

"No, it's your kid," they would tell me. I had no choice.

Now I feed her and play with her a lot. We play basketball. I take her to the park and we play kickball.

Mick, 19 - Cassandra, 25 months

Building a Family

If you're the dad, how much time do you spend with your child? Do you do your share of diaper changing and bath-giving? Do you play with him now, or are you waiting

She's helping Dad read.

until he's big enough to play football with you? If you're
the mother, do you assume you should be the one to be
with your toddler most of the time? Or would you like dad,
if he's with you, to get more involved?

Ernesta felt very strongly that mother and father should
share child care. She understood the benefits not only to
herself, but for the baby and the father. Osvaldo didn't
agree at first, but Ernesta didn't give up her dream of a
family with both parents involved with their children:

> *At first when the baby needed changing, my hus-*
> *band would say, "No, that's the mother's job."*
>
> *I'd say, "No, it's not just the mother's job. I didn't*
> *have the baby by myself. It took both of us."*
>
> *In the beginning he wouldn't help. We fought a lot*
> *about that. Finally I told his mom that he didn't want*
> *to help me do anything. His mom got mad at him and*
> *told him, "You have to help her."*
>
> *My father never helped my mom, so I grew up*
> *without any idea of how to talk to my dad. I told*
> *Osvaldo, "If you want a relationship like that, forget*
> *it. We'll just end our relationship right here. I want a*
> *family where the father is very involved." That made*
> *him think about it.*
>
> *We even went to see a counselor once, and she*
> *helped us a lot. Now he helps me, and I think it's*
> *great. I think all fathers should, not just because*
> *mothers need help, but because he has to build a*
> *relationship with the baby himself. There's mother*
> *love and father love, not just mother love for the baby.*
>
> Ernesta, 20 - Jeremy, 3; Osvaldo, Jr., 5 months

Osvaldo undoubtedly has a better relationship with his
children because of Ernesta's insistence that he share in the
child care.

Learning to Be a Father

Meghan, too, was convinced that parenting is for mothers *and* fathers. Her father was never at home as she was growing up. Tim's parents played the traditional roles of dad out working and mom home with the kids.

Meghan wanted more for their children. She and Tim didn't marry until Angel was nearly two. In fact, they split up during pregnancy, and Tim didn't see his son until Angel was five months old. From that time on, he spent a lot of time with Meghan and Angel. Meghan shared their story:

I said Tim didn't need to be with me but I wanted our son to know him. He started coming over, and he started playing daddy real quick. I showed him how to change diapers. I said, "You need to be part of his life. I'll show you how to change a diaper. You'll catch on, you will."

He was scared. He didn't know how to take care of Angel. He would always ask me what to do, and I said, "You're his father. You have to learn these things."

Once when Angel needed a bath, and I told Tim to do it, he said "No."

I said, "Why not?"

"My father never gave me a bath."

I asked him to leave. He got me upset, and I didn't want to be upset in front of Angel because I knew a baby gets upset if you're upset. Tim asked why I wanted him to leave.

I said, "You're his father and I'm his mother, and I thought we were in this 50-50. These are not the old days. Maybe your father didn't give you a bath, does that mean you can't bathe Angel? This is a whole

different situation. Maybe you had a bad childhood,
but don't take it out on Angel."
  He looked at me and said, "You're right again."
  I said, "Don't be scared. I'll be there to help you.
Nothing can happen except get him clean."
  So we worked past that one, and he started giving
Angel baths. Then he started doing just about every-
thing. His family has the old traditions. The mother is
in the kitchen and she's pregnant. She takes care of
the kids and daddy doesn't do anything with the kids.
They kind of resented that I got Tim to change.
  We agreed that whatever we do is our business.
We're a family now, so whatever they think, they can
keep their opinions to themselves.

                Meghan, 25 - Angel, 8; Kenny, 6; Jose, 2; Leon, 8 months

Keeping up with a super-active toddler is hard. As
Meghan understood so well, if two parents can share the
child care, everyone will be better off. Mother won't get so
exhausted, daddy will enjoy his child more if he's involved,
and baby, of course, will be most pleased of all.

When Dad Lives Elsewhere

Some couples stay together throughout pregnancy, but
don't get married. Many break up after the baby is born. In
fact, the majority of teenage parents, whether or not they
marry, are not together by the time their child is three, or
even two years old.

Many, like Yumiko and Marc, never live together.
During the early months of parenting, the couple may see a
great deal of each other, but their relationship eventually
ends. Where does dad fit in at this point?

Yumiko and Marc attended different high schools. Marc
was working, but he saw Yumiko nearly every day during

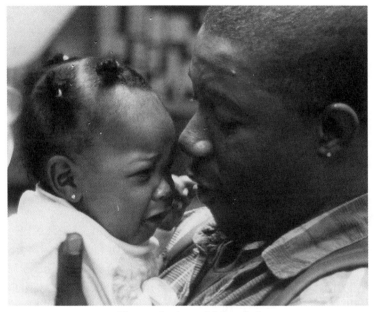

She needs time with her dad.

her pregnancy. For another year they remained close. He spent most evenings with Yumiko and Marty.

As the months went by, Yumiko realized she was growing up faster than Marc. They started fighting and finally split. Yumiko is seeing another man now. She described Marc's relationship with Marty:

> *Marc doesn't take much responsibility for Marty. I used to push him when we were together. I'd say, "You're a father now. You should do this."*
>
> *Now he doesn't come to see Marty very often. Several times he's called and said he was coming over to take Marty somewhere, and then he doesn't show up. That was disappointing for Marty. I don't feel there is any big reason for Marty to go over there.*
>
> *I think Marc feels he doesn't have to worry about seeing Marty because he'll always have some legal*

rights. I don't like the idea of him showing up when Marty is five and saying, "Hello, I'm your daddy." I think it's unfair to a kid for daddy to show up just when he feels like it.

Sometimes I feel like saying, "Go do your own thing, Marc. Don't even come over here." I can't do that, but I would think he could stop by here at least once a week. Marty was used to seeing him every day. He calls Marc "Daddy," but he doesn't really know what that means.

Yumiko, 16 - Marty, 21 months

Marc is losing out the most in this situation. He's not building a good relationship with Marty. In fact, it won't be a relationship at all if he continues ignoring his little boy.

Leila is no longer with Larissa's father. They split while Leila was pregnant, then lived together for six months after the baby was born. Then he moved out of state. A few months later he came back. Leila reported:

I'm not with Larissa's father any longer. Stewart was coming in and out of her life, but now she's old enough to be hurt by that. He's avoiding me now because I filed for paternity, and he's not cooperating.

When he came back to town the last time, I let Larissa stay with him a couple of times. Then all of a sudden he quit coming around, and I was left to answer her questions about Daddy.

I've decided if Stewart does come around, it's going to have to be a legal decision. My daughter doesn't need that, someone coming in and out of her life. I'd give anything for her to have a dad, but if he's just going to hurt her . . .

Leila, 18 - Larissa, 2 1/2

It's a dilemma. Leila would like to protect Larissa from being hurt by her father's only-occasional visits. On the other hand, will Larissa feel even more abandoned by her father if she doesn't see him at all?

Each family is different, but every effort needs to be made to help Stewart understand how disappointing it is to his daughter when he goes in and out of her life. Even if a child doesn't live with her father, she needs to know he's there and he cares about her.

Maintaining a Relationship

Many fathers who don't live with their children want a strong relationship with them. Marcus is an example:

Last night when Dorene came over, I was going out. All my friends were outside waiting for me, and here comes the mom with the baby. So I told my friends to go on because I was going to stay with my baby.

At first I was disappointed because I wanted to go out with my friends. Then Liliane ran toward me smiling, and I knew I wanted to stay with her. My baby comes first, although sometimes it's hard.

Marcus, 16 - Liliane, 15 months

Miguel lived with his daughter's mother for several months after Genny was born. In fact, if he had his way, he would still be living with his family. Since that's not possible, he spends as much time with Genny as he can:

I'll continue to keep Genny whenever I can and buy her things she needs. If I go shopping, it's not me I have on my mind, it's them, and I'll buy them something.

Today I didn't go to work so I kept Genny all day.

She's not only my daughter — she's like a little friend.
I was playing with her all day. She's all active. She
gets me tired, but I love her so much I'd do anything
for her.

She goes in all the rooms, and I have to be alert.
She's smart. She does things I wouldn't think she
would do. I'll tell her to go get me a diaper. She'll do
it, and I'll give her a hug. Every time she does
something good, I hug her.

                                        Miguel, 20 - Genny, 18 months

Your Child Changes Your Life

Miguel also talked about the changes he has made in his
life because of his daughter:

Maurine, Genny, and I lived together about six
months. It was good. I worked long hours, and then I
would see Genny. Sometimes I even worked on week-
ends, but when I didn't, I spent all my time with her.

Whenever you think you want to leave your wife or
your girlfriend, think about your child, and how you
want her to grow up. I care about myself, but I would
do anything for her. Don't ever be mean to her or
neglect her, just love her, and when she gets older,
she will give the love back to you.

I used to be in a gang, but it feels better not being
with the guys. I don't have many friends around here
any more because they're all in the gangs. If you're
older, it's not hard to get out of the gang. Me, I just
walked away. No gang has ever had control over me.
I was pressured into drugs but not to shoot this guy or
that guy. All the younger guys are like that now. I
don't want to be like that. I decided to stay off
the gangs.

I feel good about myself now. I used to be real

heavy into drugs. I stopped as soon as I started trying to get back with Maurine. I changed right away because I figured who would want someone using drugs and with the gang? There's no use getting back to her if you're going to do all that.

We fought too much. We were getting along, but I was getting jealous a lot. I don't know why. Then she decided to move out. It's different now. We're friends, and I'll continue being as close to Genny as I can.

Miguel

Having a child drastically changes the lives of fathers as well as mothers. Yes, a father can walk away, and some fathers do just that. Other fathers, like Miguel, know that dad, as well as mother, will be ahead if he truly shares the parenting responsibilities along with the joys of rearing his child. Whether or not you live with your child, the more involved you are in his life, the better your relationship will be.

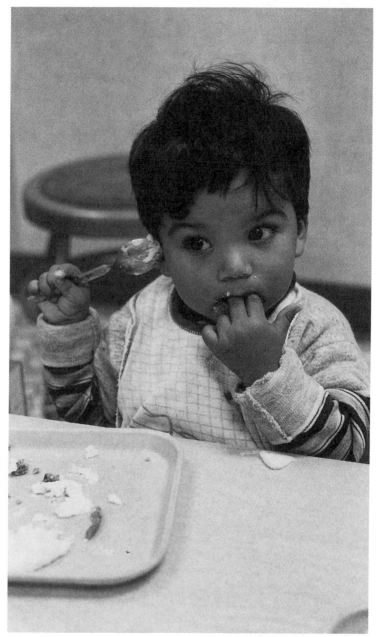

He needs less food than he did his first year.

6

Mealtime for Toddlers

- **Keeping Mealtime Pleasant**
- **She Can Eat with You**
- **Offer Small Helpings**
- **Coping with Messiness**
- **Toddler Needs Less Food**
- **Serving New Foods**
- **Outlaw Junk Food**
- **Fat-Proofing Your Toddler**
- **Extended Family Living**
- **It's Your Responsibility**

Ahmud likes to feed himself. He eats regularly, and he eats until he's full. If he puts something in his mouth and he doesn't like the taste, he spits it right out.

Between meals he only wants to eat when someone else is eating. I know if I give him too much between meals it will spoil his appetite. He's been on table food most of the time since he was ten months old, and he hasn't had allergic reactions to anything. He usually eats whatever we eat.

We eat at home more than we eat out. If we go out to eat, I try to find something good for them.

Mary, 21 - Shawna, 4; Ahmud, 20 months

Keeping Mealtime Pleasant

Many adults consider eating an enjoyable pastime. Some of us enjoy it too much! But for many small children, mealtime becomes a hassle, a fight with mother and dad.

"Eat your meat right now."

"Just one more bite of green beans."

"No dessert for you until you finish your carrots!"

A toddler's mealtime doesn't have to be a bad experience for everyone. Toddlers have the same kinds of food needs as the rest of us. They need nutritious foods from the Food Pyramid groups. (See *Your Baby's First Year.*) They also need a relaxed, friendly atmosphere at mealtime. Both needs are important, as Esteban points out:

> *Nathan eats pretty good. He likes vegetables. I used to get all nervous trying to feed him, and it seems to me the kid knows when you're nervous, and you just get more nervous. Instead, you want to make it fun while they eat.*
>
> Esteban, 18 - Nathan, 2; Ralph, 5 months

She Can Eat With You

By now, your child can probably eat her meals with you. With a little planning, most of your easy-to-chew food should be suitable for her. Cut meat, fish, and vegetables into bite-size cubes.

If you're frying food for your family, it's better for your toddler if you broil or dry-fry her food in a non-stick pan. Serve her food before you add the spices or the rich sauce. Foods to avoid completely at this age include popcorn and nuts or any food that might cause her to choke.

> *Susie eats everything in sight. She's a little pig. She's never been finicky. I think it's because everyone else eats everything. We never had a problem with her*

eating. We don't let her drink a lot of soda, and she's allergic to milk, so we give her the Lactaid which is a liquid she drinks with every meal.

She often eats two helpings of dinner. She loves hamburger. Food has never been a battle, and I think that has a lot to do with grandma. Up here we don't have that many fast-food places, so we do a lot of home cooking.

Cathi, 18 - Susie, 34 months

Convenience foods such as canned soups are not as nutritious as foods you prepare yourself. Soups and other dehydrated meals usually contain more salt than your child should have. These foods also contain a variety of preservatives, colorings, and artificial flavorings. It's all right to serve them occasionally, but a steady diet of already-prepared foods is not especially good for any of us. Neither is a steady diet of fast-foods.

Offer Small Helpings

Give her small helpings of food. Don't worry if she doesn't seem to eat much. She doesn't need as much as she did six months ago when she was growing so much faster than she is now. She needs daily:

- Twenty ounces of milk
- Fruits and vegetables
- Bread and cereal
- Protein foods

If she doesn't drink enough milk, put it in puddings and soups. Does she like cheese? Let cheese take the place of some of her milk. Cottage cheese and yogurt are also good replacements.

While most toddlers insist on feeding themselves, you may find she occasionally insists just as strongly that you feed her. That's all right. She may not be feeling well, or she may simply be tired of feeding herself all the time.

Allow plenty of time for your toddler to eat. Rushing through a meal is not her style. She'll eat many foods with her fingers, but by her second birthday, she'll be able to handle a spoon quite well.

Coping with Messiness

When Derek eats and he's through, he's through. You'd better get him down fast —or he'll throw his food and jump out of his high chair!

Laurette, 17 - Derek, 18 months

*Toddlers do **not** eat neatly!*

Learning to use a spoon is hard work and takes a lot of practice. He has to try. If mother insists on neatness at the table, he'll be discouraged. While he's learning, it's impossible for him to be neat.

When he eats a cracker, he may first gum it.

Then he'll rub the mess all over his face and into his hair. There is no reason to let him sit on the couch while he makes this mess, of course, but his high chair can be cleaned up.

Put a thick layer of newspapers on the floor under his chair to catch the spills. Roll them up after dinner and throw them away. Then you have only your toddler and his chair to clean.

He is fairly easily washed, although he may not appreciate your efforts. If you give him a second washcloth to use on himself while you clean him up, it may help. Try not to let the mess upset you.

Some parents are so horrified at the mess their toddler makes while eating that they don't want anyone else around at mealtime. That's okay.

Because of the mess, some people feed toddlers before the rest of the family eats. This is undoubtedly better than scolding the child throughout dinner for his absolutely normal messiness.

If you realize how normal this messiness is, and that it will happen at this age, you can probably handle it without too much frustration.

By now, your child will probably be drinking most of his milk from a cup or small glass. If you fill it only one-fourth full, the inevitable spilling will be less of a disaster. You can refill it one-fourth full as often as he wants it. Be sure you encourage him to drink plenty of milk.

Toddler Needs Less Food

Remember that your toddler's appetite is much less than it was. She's not growing nearly as fast as she did those first twelve months. It is during this stage that many mothers decide their toddlers are "terrible eaters." "She just doesn't eat a thing," they say.

Meghan is not a good eater. She practically won't touch anything. All she wants is a glass of milk constantly, and it worries me. I told the doctor about it. She laughed and said, "Oh, I can tell you're going through the fun stage."

"What can I do about it?" I asked. She said to give Meghan vitamins with iron, and that seemed to help her appetite. She also told me to quit fussing about it.

I try to avoid candy because I don't like to give them too many sweets. Sometimes when Meghan doesn't want to eat, I think it's because she's too busy to bother. She does love pizza.

Louise, 19 - Meghan, 23 months; Mark, 5 months

Don't try to force or even coax her to eat. Offer small servings of nutritious food. Don't offer sweets at all. If she seems to need an in-between-meal snack, make it part of her daily food plan. Carrots, orange juice, graham crackers, milk, and apple are examples of good snack foods that won't pave the way for your lovely child to become a fat adult. If you overfeed now, remember, she is likely to have a weight problem when she's grown. You don't want your child to spend her life fighting unhealthy, unattractive fat.

Sean snacks a lot —plums, grapes, nectarines, peaches. He doesn't eat much candy and other sweets. I won't let him. He doesn't need any candy because of his teeth, and because it would spoil his appetite.

Ginger, 18 - Sean, 17 months

If she doesn't want to eat any lunch at all, calmly take her food away. She won't starve by suppertime. Just don't tide her over with a handful of cookies an hour later.

If she eats all her food and asks for more, give it to her in the same way, without an emotional reaction. Whether she eats all her food or not is not what makes her a "good girl."

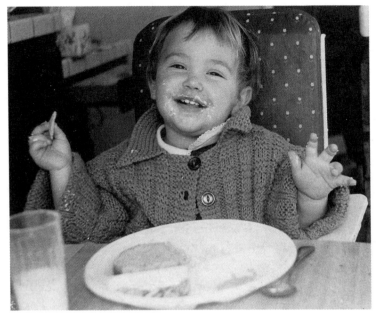

It's important that she enjoy mealtime.

Serving New Foods

There are a lot of things he won't eat. He doesn't like vegetables. I put them on his plate every night, but if he doesn't eat, I don't force it. My mother is more like, "You have to make him eat," but I don't.

Jessica, 17 - Craig, 2½

Your toddler may appear to like only a few foods. When you offer him a new food, he may refuse even to taste it. Rather than insisting he "clean his plate," serve yourself the same food and show him you like to eat it. Suggest that he might taste it. If he refuses, however, it's okay. There's no need to bribe, force, or push.

Research shows that children who are bribed to eat new foods are less likely to eat that food later than are those who simply are served the food with no bribe involved.

Serve the new food again a few days later. He may be willing to try it, but don't make a fuss if he doesn't. Absolutely nothing is accomplished when mom or dad demands that the child eat the food.

Your child is in control at this point. *You, however, are in control of the foods served.* You don't need to serve soda or other junk foods in your home.

Continue offering her the variety of foods the rest of your family is eating. You may say she won't eat any vegetables at all. What about raw ones? She can get even more vitamins from raw vegetables than from cooked ones.

Until she's two, however, don't give her raw carrot sticks or other hard-to-chew foods because she might choke. If she likes raw carrots, grate them for her.

Hot dogs may be an all-American food, but they really shouldn't be given to toddlers because of the risk of choking. Even if you slit the skin or slice them into little circles, your child could choke on a piece of hot dog. Besides, hot dogs are high in fat.

Meals and snacks need to be at about the same time every day. Toddlers have small stomachs, and they get hungry within a couple of hours after a meal. If he refuses to eat at mealtime, then asks for a snack immediately afterward, it's generally best not to give it to him. Tell him he must wait until snack time.

Sometimes he may refuse foods he's liked before. This happened with Lorenzo. Guadalupe and Domingo handled the situation very well:

For awhile Lorenzo wasn't eating very well. He didn't like a lot of foods — he was very very picky. First it was eggs, then enchiladas, then meat, then broccoli. Every time I cooked something, it was, "I don't like that."

Well, I didn't make him eat it. I would ask why he didn't like this because he used to eat it. He would just say, "Because I don't like them any more." So I wasn't going to make him eat it. I'd ask him if he wanted some soup, and he'd say "Yes," and I would give him soup.

Then one day Domingo got up and made Lorenzo some eggs and some meat, and he ate it. We were amazed. I guess a little time passed . . . Now he eats all those foods again.

I know a kid would never appreciate you forcing him to eat. He'd withdraw more. I never want to force him to do something he doesn't want to do if he doesn't really need to do it.

Guadalupe, 20 - Lorenzo, 4

If Lorenzo's parents had made a big fuss each time he refused a food, and had insisted that he eat it, he probably would have become more firmly convinced he didn't like those foods. Because they didn't let his temporary food dislikes become a battle between them and their son, Lorenzo grew out of this food-refusing phase.

Outlaw Junk Food

Leah likes grilled cheese sandwiches, macaroni, chicken soup. She eats the same stuff we do, and usually she eats pretty well. When she doesn't eat much, it's usually when she's tired.

Every time I go anywhere with anyone, though, it's "Can Leah have some ice cream?" or "Can Leah have a cookie?" It's not just that I don't want her to have this stuff, but I know how she acts — ten minutes later she's real hyper. If she gets a couple of drinks of pop, she runs around wild. Usually I give her stuff without chocolate because it's the caffeine that makes her crazy.

Lyra, 18 - Leah, 2½

"Junk food" is food which contains very few nutrients but which is very high in fat, sugar, and calories. You aren't getting much nutrition at all when you eat junk foods such as potato chips, French fries, shakes, hot dogs, lunch meats, cookies, candy, doughnuts, and soft drinks.

Keep the junk food away from your picky eater. If he isn't hungry enough for meals, he certainly doesn't need a soda, potato chips, or even cookies an hour later. While one or two oatmeal cookies provide a little nutrition, a handful of sugary snacks won't do much for him except ruin his appetite for more nutritious foods.

If you're in your own home, or if the people you live with are willing, don't keep junk food there at all. If you don't have candy and cookies in the cupboard or soft drinks in the refrigerator, your toddler can't have them while he's at home. The occasional sweet he gets from the outside world won't matter that much as long as you aren't providing them, too.

She has always eaten good. I let her munch if she wants to —whole wheat and peanut butter crackers, but no junk at all. I used to have problems with my teeth, and I don't want her to.

I think junk food is so bad for you. I used to always eat stuff like that. No cokes. My doctor said if you pour coke on a car, it will eat the paint right off!

Ione, 18 - Lori, 14 months

Fat-Proofing Your Toddler

If you have a toddler who already appears overweight, don't put him on a reducing diet. Do, however, guide his eating so that he gains weight more slowly. Make a list of the food he eats in a three-day period. You may be surprised at the amount of high-calorie food he consumes.

Don't cut out the meat, vegetables, milk, fruit, and cereal, his Food Pyramid foods. Get serious about not having junk food in the house. If he drinks more than a quart of milk a day, try diluting it with water. Most doctors don't recommend skim or low-fat milk for children under two.

Encourage your overweight toddler to get more exercise. Do you take walks, but push him in his stroller? Get him to walk with you. Is he outdoors enough? It may take extra energy on your part to get him to a park if you don't have a yard, but it may well be worth the effort.

Both Dawn and her daughter, Mercedes, 3, are quite overweight. Dawn's food habits probably explain both her own and her daughter's weight problem. Like all children, Mercedes mimics her mother. She, too, eats a lot of junk food, then is "picky," as her mother says, at mealtime.

I'm a big junk food eater, a nervous eater, and I pick all the time. A lot of foods you're supposed to have I don't even like. I like my bacon, fried potatoes, toast and butter, the eggs — but they have to be done in grease. For lunch I seldom just make sandwiches for us. It's McDonald's. If we don't eat breakfast we usually go to McDonald's, and then have something here. We do hit the ice cream man.

Mercedes doesn't eat enough to do anything. In the morning she'll have a bowl of cereal or a couple of pieces of bacon. She doesn't like eggs and doesn't care much for potatoes.

At lunch if we go to McDonald's she'll eat half of a half of a hamburger, plus a half bag of fries, maybe

*half of her drink. With dinner she will eat at the most
ten tiny squares of meat.*

Dawn Ellen, 19 - Mercedes, 3

Even at McDonalds, Dawn Ellen's cost for food is fairly
high, but she isn't getting much for her money. Mercedes is
growing and developing at a rapid rate, and desperately
needs better nutrition. Fruits and vegetables should be a
large part of Mercedes' diet. Yet they're completely

Toddlers need nutritious and easy-to-eat foods.

missing except for French fries. Neither is she getting any milk.

Mark and Kelly Ellen were eating a lot of junk food. When they realized that Dustin was copying their poor food habits, they decided to change their ways. Mark explained:

For three or four months Dustin had cola all the time. He'd go through all the sodas. The same with Twinkies and cakes. We were drinking a lot of cola and had potato chips everywhere.

Then we realized all that junk food was getting expensive and we were both gaining weight, so we started a little diet. Now we don't even buy sodas. Now we're real conscious about what we eat, and the same goes for him.

For the last year or so, we won't give him junk food. We learned from experience. If he has candy all day, he gets higher and crankier.

Junk food is like a lot of other things. If it's there and it's annoying, just take it away. As you take it away, explain why he can't have it. If we had a box full of cakes and cookies, he'd be into it. So we stopped having junk in the house.

Mark, 22 - Dustin, 2½

Nutrition and Extended Family Living

A surprising number of young parents talked about their concern because grandma thinks the baby should have candy and other foods his mother doesn't believe are good for him.

Janis doesn't like to eat a whole lot, or even at all sometimes. So my mom will resort to sweet cereal so she'll eat. I know if you wait until she's hungry, she'll eat what we have.

*They give her ice cream and candy, and she's
going to get cavities too soon. My mom says, "She
needs something in her stomach," but all it is
is sugar.*

Darla, 17 - Janis, 2

*Shelly doesn't snack a lot except when she sees
somebody eating something. She has very little candy.
First of all, she makes a mess, and besides, I don't
want her to get cavities. I don't give her soft drinks
either, just orange juice or apple juice.*

*Everybody tells me, "You're so mean, you don't
give her any candy. When she gets older, she's going
to see all that candy and eat it all."*

*Even my mother tells me I'm so mean. She makes
herself sound like she knows more than I do. She used
to always give candy to Shelly behind my back.*

*One time they were eating chocolates, and I told
Shelly she couldn't have any. Then she walked by me,
and she had chocolate all over her mouth. It makes
me feel bad.*

*I feel like telling them to mind their own business,
but I can't do that. Mom's beginning to do more of
that, and it's getting to me. It's building up, and I
know I'll wind up telling her something I shouldn't.*

Dixie, 18 - Shelly, 17 months

If this is happening in your home, perhaps you could try
talking with your family. Could you work out a change? If
your family doesn't know much about nutrition, perhaps
you could tactfully provide some help on the subject of
feeding toddlers. There are lots of well-written and brief
pamphlets as well as whole books on this topic.

Do you eat a lot of junk food? If you set a good example
for your child by eating mostly nutritious foods, your

family may be more likely to respect your wishes concerning your child's nutrition.

If you aren't already doing much of the food preparation, could you offer to help more with the understanding that your child is not to be given junk food?

Of course, you know your family, and you can probably come up with better ideas for changing the situation.

It's Your Responsibility

You have three basic responsibilities connected with feeding your child:

- You need to offer him the nutritious food he needs.
- Help him learn that mealtime is a pleasant, sociable time. It's not a period of coaxing him to eat, or a time to argue with the rest of the family.
- Help him stay at a healthy weight.

Your modeling is all important in the development of your toddler's food habits. If you're a picky eater, or if you survive mostly on junk food, you can expect your child to do the same thing. If you're careful to eat foods from the Food Pyramid groups at each meal, your child is more likely to eat well, too.

When this happens, payoff is high in terms of your toddler's health and general development. Her disposition is likely to be better, too, because she'll feel better if she eats the foods she needs.

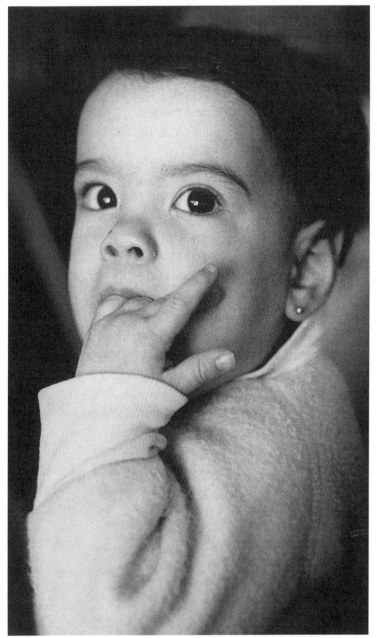

A bedtime ritual with Mom or Dad helps prevent bedtime problems.

7

Importance
of Sleep

• Sleep/Rest
  for Toddlers
• Importance
  of Bedtime Ritual
• Solving Bedtime
  Problems
• She Doesn't Want
  to Be Alone
• Every-Five-Minutes
  Routine
• Night Waking
• Should Child Sleep
  with Parent?
• Crowded Home
  Affects Sleeping
  Habits
• Remember —
  Routine Helps

Juanito has slept through the entire night since he was three months old. He likes to have a glass of chocolate milk before he goes to bed, a bedtime story, and then to bed by 9:30.

Sometimes it's hard because I want to watch TV, but he won't go to sleep if I do. So I turn off the TV and make everything dark for thirty minutes, and he goes to sleep.

Kashira, 19 - Juanito, 4

Ellie usually goes to bed at 7:30 or 8:00. It's not like whenever she goes to bed, it's okay. It's better for her to have a schedule.

*She doesn't fight me. She knows when she has to go
to bed. I help her with her PJs, brush her teeth, then
usually lie down and talk with her or read a book, or
tell her what we'll do the next morning.*

                                   Shalimar, 19 - Ellie, 21/2

Sleep/Rest Important for Toddlers

Your toddler will be less cranky if she eats and sleeps, or
at least rests, at regular times. You also need time for
yourself. Her daytime naps help both of you.

Most toddlers continue taking a fairly long afternoon
nap. Some, however, may not want to nap. It's best to put
her to bed anyway, together with her favorite stuffed toy
and some books. If she doesn't go to sleep, an hour of quiet
play will refresh her for the rest of the day.

Generally, toddlers don't have a particularly difficult
time getting to sleep at night. Now that they get around
easily, they fill their day with activity. By evening they're
usually tired and ready for sleep. However, this isn't always the case. Sleep problems can occur at any age.

Sometimes at around a year, a baby who was fairly easy
to get down for sleep may suddenly start having a difficult
time. He may resist everything about getting ready for bed.
At this age, he enjoys being with his parents, and he
doesn't want to leave them. He doesn't want to be alone.

When toddlers hit the "I'll do it myself" stage, complete
with lots of "No," bedtime may once again become a
problem.

*Bedtime is a hassle. Henry won't go to bed before I
do, and he won't go in his crib. For the last couple of
months, he has been in bed with me. If I put him in his
crib, he cries and climbs out of it. He goes to sleep
with me, then I put him in his crib.*

He has his bath after he eats dinner. I put his pajamas on him and get him ready for bed. Then he wants to go outside, and he gets all dirty again.

He goes to bed when we do, but at 6:30 in the morning he doesn't want to get up. Today I brought him to school asleep. I couldn't wake him up.

He used to go to bed earlier. I think the change was when he quit taking a bottle and started playing outside more.

Olivia, 20 - Henry, 23 months

Henry is like most toddlers. He's so busy playing and learning about his world that he doesn't want to take time to sleep. His parents should decide on the time they feel he should be in bed, then see that he gets there at that time.

Getting Henry ready for bed, then allowing him to go outside to play doesn't help him settle down to sleep. If they bathe him a little later and develop a more elaborate bedtime routine with him, he may fall asleep more easily.

Importance of Bedtime Ritual

Before he goes to bed, Dalton watches one of those animal videos for about thirty minutes. Then we play with him for thirty minutes, we brush his teeth, and we read several books to him. Sometimes he likes to have his head or his back or his stomach rubbed.

I work three or four nights a week, so if I'm not home, Dalton's dad goes through all this with him. It works pretty well.

Claire, 17 - Dalton, 33 months

Parents often start a bedtime routine when their child is six or eight months old. They find it helps their child settle down to sleep without a lot of fussing. If this isn't working as well now, the solution may be an even more complicated bedtime ritual.

Quiet play, a little snack, a relaxing bath, and looking at a book, with perhaps a lullaby or two, might be a part of your child's ritual for falling asleep. Turning on a night light or some soft music may help, too. One little girl had a certain corner of her blanket which she rubbed on her cheek while she sucked her thumb. To her parent's amazement, she could find that one corner even in the dark. Lots of toddlers need that special blanket when they go to bed:

> *Derek sometimes drives me up the wall when he won't go to sleep. He has this one blanket that he has to have to go to bed. He's had it all his life. Everybody calls him Linus.*
>
> *I'll say, "Where's your blanket?" and he'll go get it.*
>
> Laurette, 17 - Derek, 18 months

Six months ago, perhaps you read to her, rocked her a few minutes, and put her to bed with her teddy bear. Now she has to have a drink before she kisses you, not after. She may want the same story every night. Perhaps she has to tell each toy "Night-night." Whatever her routine, woe to you if you upset it!

This ritual, if she feels she's in charge, can be a good compromise. You get what you want when she goes to bed without a huge fuss. You each give up something, too. You take the time to go through the ritual with her, and she goes to bed. So don't try to get out of that bedtime story once in awhile just because you're tired. It's important to her.

Solving Bedtime Problems

If your child already has a problem going to bed, the solution may not be easy. One young mother, whose husband recently joined the Navy, moved in with her

Her favorite doll helps her settle down to sleep.

parents-in-law for two months. She then decided she and her daughter would be better off in their own home. But Esperanza's child didn't adapt to coming back home as well as she had hoped:

> *Juanita is a crybaby. She is really spoiled because I've been at Ruben's mother's house. She got a lot of attention there.*
>
> *When I came back home, I couldn't give her that much attention because I have to do a lot of things here. She won't stay in her crib to take a nap. She just screams. I either take her out and set her here in the living room, or I leave her in there and she screams.*
>
> *She used to sleep three or four hours each afternoon. Over there she would sleep only 45 minutes or so. Before, she was always happy, but now she isn't. She has changed, and I don't understand why.*

*When Juanita was four months old, I got real
attached to her because Ruben was gone. I always
had her by me, and I spent my whole time with her.
She hates that crib now, but I hate to put her on my
bed. She sleeps with me a lot. When Ruben comes
home, I guess I'll have to let her sleep with us.
I should start getting her used to the crib and let
her cry.*

Esperanza, 17 - Juanita, 12 months

Juanita has had more change than she likes in her first
year of living. First, daddy was home. Then he left. Then
Juanita and mother moved in with a family consisting of
grandma, grandpa, and several young aunts and uncles.
Now she's back in the apartment with her mother and her
other grandma who is gone most of the time.

She's not sure what's going on in her world. First, she
needs a terrific amount of love from mother. But mother is
lonely and unhappy because daddy is gone. It's a difficult
situation any way you look at it.

If Esperanza really wants Juanita to sleep in her crib,
perhaps she should insist, and insist over and over again,
that Juanita sleep there. At the same time, Esperanza needs
to spend much more time with Juanita and try extra hard to
help her feel secure again.

She Doesn't Want to Be Alone

If a baby cries when she's put to bed, it's probably
because she doesn't want to be there. She doesn't want to
be there because she doesn't want to be alone. She would
far rather stay out in the living room with her parents. She
may feel a bit deserted when she's in bed by herself and
mom or dad has shut the door firmly.

One "solution" often tried when baby cries is to get her

up again, hoping that in time she will quiet down enough to go to sleep. With this method, she gets to be up with you. She learns that if she cries, she can get up. Why should she go to bed tomorrow night without fussing?

The opposite "solution" is to shut the door even more firmly and leave her alone to cry. A few minutes of crying won't hurt her. If she's tired enough, she'll go to sleep, exactly what you want.

Some toddlers, however, will cry and cry for a couple of hours if left alone. They may fall asleep from exhaustion, but they're not likely to sleep well after such an ordeal. This is the kind of crying Esperanza described. Her solution was to let Juanita sleep with her on her bed. But that wasn't the solution Esperanza wanted.

Every-Five-Minutes Routine

A sensible approach, if your child is at least ten months old, could be a combination of the first two methods. When she cries, go in to see her. Tell her "Good night," pat her back a minute, then walk out. If she continues crying, repeat the process five minutes later. Continue going back in to reassure her every five minutes until she goes to sleep.

She may cry for another hour, but she knows you haven't left her because she's seen you every five minutes. She also knows she won't be brought back into the living room after bedtime.

This method, according to Penelope Leach, author of *Your Baby and Child from Birth to Age Five* (1997: Alfred A. Knopf), will almost always work. Within a week at the most, your toddler should be much more accepting of her bedtime.

Why make such a fuss? Why not let her stay up until she decides she's ready to go to bed? As mentioned before, most toddlers become utterly exhausted before they will give in to sleep. A tired toddler is often a miserable toddler.

A young mother in our school's parenting class described the problem she was having in getting her 14-month-old son to go to bed and to sleep at night. He would get up again and again. He wouldn't go to sleep until very late. In desperation, she often allowed him to stay up far longer than was good for him or for his parents.

I suggested she try the go-in-every-five-minutes-and-pat-his-back routine as a possible solution.

Two days later Jamie returned to report that the every-five-minutes routine had worked. She added, "I was so exhausted after those first two nights I couldn't get up to come to school!" The third night, she said, Austin was asleep twenty minutes after she put him to bed.

Toddlers may sleep better if the day includes active outdoor play.

Night Waking

*Lorenzo sleeps very well, but every once in awhile
he used to wake up with a nightmare. He'd say he's
getting chased by monsters. I would hear him crying,
and I'd get up and try to wake him up enough to get
him out of his dream.*

Guadalupe, 20 - Lorenzo, 4

Your toddler may have a nightmare occasionally. After
he's asleep, you hear him screaming. When you go in, he
may be kicking or moving frantically. He needs you to
reassure him that you're there, that it was only a bad dream.

Go in and talk to him for a minute. Perhaps he would
like a drink of water. When he calms down and isn't afraid
anymore, tell him "Good night" and go back to bed.

Occasionally young mothers spoke of giving their year-
old children several bottles during the night. If he has a
bottle at bedtime, he doesn't need the extra food. Again,
remember the danger of tooth decay if your child sleeps
with a bottle of milk.

If he wakes, instead of handing him a bottle, offer him a
cup of water. Tell him "Good night" and walk away. If he
continues crying, try the every-five-minutes routine for a
week. You'll be exhausted, but if he starts sleeping through
the night, think how much better you'll feel the next week.

Should Child Sleep with Parent?

*Donovan has always slept in his crib in his own
room. But now he's starting to cry and cry when he
goes to bed.*

*I lie down with him for awhile, but lately he wants
to sleep with me. I want him to learn he has a bed,
and that's where he sleeps.*

Belia, 17 - Donovan, 2

"Should" you sleep with your child? Most child development experts in our culture say "No." Some people, however, believe otherwise. Some parents feel it's easier to sleep with their toddler. Perhaps they just like having the child sleep in bed with them. As long as everyone is able to sleep well, it doesn't seem to matter.

However, there may be some problems. One parent or the other may not be able to get enough rest. Then, of course, there is the issue of privacy. Children should not observe lovemaking.

Also, once this pattern has become established, it may be very difficult to stop. Having their child sleep with them was described as a problem by several of the young parents interviewed.

One thing I did that I wish I hadn't was letting Heidi sleep with me. When she was little, a newborn, I took her to bed with me. She didn't like her crib very much. She would sleep with me all night, and my mom would say, "You have to put her in that crib or she won't ever sleep in it."

She was right. At about five months, I put her in her crib and let her sleep by herself. She didn't like that at all, but after a couple of weeks she was okay. Dennis feels pretty strong about not wanting Heidi to sleep with us.

I have a suggestion for mothers of newborns. If they breastfeed and have the child in bed with them, they should, after they feed him, put him in his own bed.

Jenny, 18 - Heidi, 13 months

Crowded Home Affects Sleeping Habits

Sometimes the fact that the house is more crowded because of the baby creates extra problems. Grandma may want the same rules followed that she remembers using when her children were little. If the baby must share a room with other family members, things get complicated:

> *My mom doesn't bug me, but she's making me feel like I don't know what I'm doing, like I'm a little kid. For example, Shelly never got used to the crib.*
>
> *She's in a room with my cousin, and they keep coming in and out, turning on the light, and waking her. So I pick her up and take her in where I sleep, but my mom says I'll have problems later on.*
>
> *I tell her I can't help it, that I have to get some sleep so I can go to school. She'll sleep there for about two hours, but not the whole night.*
>
> *If Shelly had the room by herself, I would let her alone.*
>
> Dixie, 18 - Shelly, 17 months

Dixie appears to have worked out a rather good solution. Perhaps she needs to share with her mom her reasons for moving Shelly into her room. She might even consider moving Shelly's crib into her room.

It's nice if parent and child can have separate rooms, but often this isn't possible. Shelly might be able to go to sleep more easily if she is routinely put in her crib in Dixie's room. Expecting a toddler to sleep while other children go in and out of the room is expecting a lot.

Sometimes a mother feels she has no choice but to sleep with her baby. There's no room otherwise.

> *Gary wakes up about three times each night. I give him a bottle and change him. He sleeps with me.*
>
> *I had no choice. I didn't want him to, but we moved here when he was about 1 1/2 months old, and there was no place for the crib. I had to store it away, so he*

*slept with me. Then a month ago my sister moved out,
and there was room for the crib. I put it up the other
day, but he won't sleep in it.*

   *He is really attached to me at night. He won't go to
sleep until I do. I hope he outgrows it.*

Jan, 15 - Gary, 12 months

Although Gary has already formed a strong habit of
sleeping with his mother, Jan has three choices. She can
continue letting him sleep with her. Perhaps he will eventually outgrow it, as she hopes. The danger here is that his
mother may suddenly decide at a later time that she doesn't
want him in bed with her. It may be even harder to get him
to sleep elsewhere then.

   She can let him go to sleep in her bed, then move him to
his crib. If she chooses this method, she should tell him
what she will be doing. She might say, "You may go to
sleep in my bed. After you're asleep, I'll move you into
your own bed where you will sleep the rest of the night."

   Another solution is to insist he sleep in his crib now. Jan
could follow the check-on-him-every-five-minutes routine
described previously. It will be difficult both for her and for
Gary, but it might be worth the effort.

   Brigette found a fairly simple solution to a similar
problem:

   *Rudy has slept with me at least three-fourths of his
life. It got to the point where he wouldn't go to sleep
until I was in bed with him. I would lie down with him
for about an hour until he was asleep. I strongly
recommend you not sleep with your kids — except
when they're sick, of course.*

   *Now I'll be marrying John, and I don't want Rudy
to think John is kicking him out of my bed. A friend
suggested I get him a new bed and make a big deal of*

it. She said I should do this long before my wedding.
Then when I get married, it will all be done.
I bought Rudy a youth bed. He was thrilled, and it
worked. He goes to sleep by himself in his own
bed now.

Brigette, 22 - Joy, 4; Rudy, 3

Remember — Routine Helps

Helping her learn to eat and sleep at regular hours is
almost certain to improve your child's disposition. In fact,
the "spoiled" toddler who whines a lot and is generally
demanding may improve a great deal if she is put on a
reasonable time schedule.

With careful planning and your willingness to develop a
bedtime routine for your child and to stick to that routine
every night, bedtime can be a pleasant experience for you
and your child. It can be a time of special closeness
between you, a time you both may cherish.

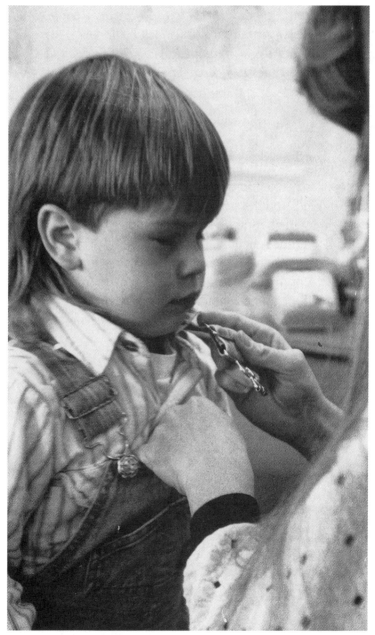

She's growing up — but she still needs your help occasionally.

8

Your Amazing
Two-Year-Old

- New World
  of Learning
- Her First Teacher
- "I Love You,
  Mommy"
- To Bed, To Sleep?
- No Mealtime
  Arguments
- "Where Do Babies
  Come From?"
- Potty Training
- Hard to Accept
  Change
- Even More Patience
  Needed
- Winning — For
  Both of You
- You're His Model

Johnnie's not a little baby any-more — he's his own little self. He has his own personality. He doesn't like me to do things for him now, and he's more demand-ing. If he wants it, he wants it now.

I was waiting for him to talk, and now he won't stop. He wants to know about a lot of things.

You know how when they're little, they want you to carry them. Now he doesn't want me to grab him. Now he wants to walk. Sometimes I feel sad because he doesn't want me to do a lot of things.

He mimics me a lot. When I do

*my homework, he wants his pencil and his book, and
he sits down with me. I'm also watching my language
now. If I use a bad word, he's sure to repeat it.*

Natalie, 17 - Johnnie, 26 months

New World of Learning

*School is important, but it's not more important
than Leah. If Leah says she wants to sit with me or
play with me, and that means I won't get all my
homework done, I'll do it. The important thing is to
listen to your child and spend time with her. You can't
have so much to do that you can't play with her or
talk with her. You have to manage your time.*

Lyra, 18 - Leah, 2 1/2

A whole new world opens up to your toddler between
her second and third birthdays. She not only has learned to
walk and run, but is mastering other skills. She can jump,
and she can ride a variety of wheel toys. She is beginning
to dress and undress herself. She feeds herself with a little
help, and she plays with toys in a much more complex
manner. She is fond of crayons and painting.

She loves to imitate the activities of both adults and
other children. She will imitate both the way you do want
her to behave, and the way you don't want her to behave.

She can talk, and is learning new words rapidly. She
understands most of what is said to her if it is spoken in
simple terms, but she won't always interpret it correctly.
Her experience with language is limited. She may appear
defiant because she doesn't understand what you want.

Your Child's First Teacher

*I read to Leah a lot. She opens the book and reads
to herself, too, and she talks to her baby dolls.*

Leah talks like a three- or four-year-old, real well.
I think it's because we talk to her and read to her that
she talks so well. She didn't just wake up one day and
start talking like that.

Lyra

Do you plan to be a teacher? Whether your answer is yes
or no, you're one already. You are your child's first and
certainly most important teacher. If he has been in an infant
center or is attending preschool, you have help with your
teaching job. You still probably have your child with you
during a greater part of his day than do his other teachers.
You mean more to your child than any other teacher, too.

She's real bright. She's always wanting to learn
and know things. She's always asking "Why?" I try to
explain to her so she can understand.
She watches everything I do now, and she copies
me. I brush my hair, and she wants to brush hers. She
wants to brush her teeth when I do mine.

Shalimar, 19 - Ellie, 2 1/2

As he explores, talk with him. Comment on the things
around him. When you go for a walk with him, give him
a bag to collect treasures — a little rock, a feather, a
dandelion. When you return home, talk with him about
these items. Now you can also begin to talk about what
happened yesterday and your plans for tomorrow because
he's beginning to understand the idea of time.

Read to Him Again and Again

At night they pick out the books they want to read
and I read to them. Shawna kind of knows what the
story is because she almost always picks out the same
books every night. Her favorites are the Dr. Seuss

She loves to play with Mommy.

books. Before I turn the light off she wants to look at the book herself.

Ever since she was little, before she could even talk, I've taken her to the library when they have the reading programs. I started when she was six months old.

Ahmud gets jealous when he sees me reading, so now he sits down and listens, too. Sometimes he gets bored and goes off and looks at his own book. Then he'll come back and want me to read.

Mary, 21 - Shawna, 4; Ahmud, 20 months

Reading regularly, again and again, to your child is important for his and your enjoyment. It's also an important part of helping his brain develop well.

Whether or not you have books at home for your child, visit your public library together. Find out about the library's storytime for toddlers. Some libraries even have storytime for infants.

Help your toddler learn early that libaries are great places. That's where he can check out books that, first, you'll read to him. When he's older, he'll be reading to you.

Mary explained why she reads to Shawna every night whether or not she feels like it:

> *Sometimes when I'm tired, I'd just as soon not read, but I don't want them to think if you're tired you don't read. So we read anyway. When they're in school they can't quit reading just because they're tired.*
>
> Mary

Developing language skills is perhaps your child's most important task this year. You help her each time you talk with her, sing to her, tell her stories, and read to her. You also help her when you listen to her. Encourage her to tell you stories. Ask her to tell you about the book you've been reading to her every night for the past month. You may find she has it memorized! Of course you don't expect her to actually read for several years yet.

Watching and listening to your child as she develops speaking ability is exciting. Remember the baby who could only communicate with you by crying? She's come a long way!

"I Love You, Mommy"

You probably are thrilled when your toddler says "I love you." All parents like those words. Toddlers, however, are emotional little people whose feelings change quickly. The "I love you, Mommy" may turn into "I hate you" ten minutes later because you couldn't allow him to do something he wanted to do. You probably will feel hurt or angry the first time this happens.

Mickey says "No" and tells me I'm not his friend any more. I tell him I'm his friend and I still love him. He will say "No, you're not my friend," and walk away. A few minutes later he comes back and decides we're friends.

Susan, 20 - Mickey, 2 1/2; Felicia, 11 months

Instead of showing your anger, reassure him that you love him a lot and you're sorry he's feeling that way right now. Of course you won't let him kick or hurt you when he's angry — or any other time. Give him a chance to talk about his feelings if he wants to. Your patience and calm reaction will help him deal with his anger.

To Bed, to Sleep?

Fatigue is another factor that influences behavior. Toddlers are very active and tire quickly. Many resist napping. Simple fatigue and disruption of her normal sleeping schedule is at the root of many behavior problems. Recognizing this and adjusting expectations may make life easier for everyone.

If your child doesn't go right to sleep when she goes to bed, it doesn't necessarily mean she doesn't need to rest. Most two-year-olds will be better off if they continue their afternoon naps.

If she doesn't want to go to sleep, tell her that it's all right. She can play quietly in her bed. Give her some books and a quiet toy. Ask her to play there for an hour. She might like a timer set so she can get up when it dings. Chances are she'll go to sleep. If she doesn't, she will still get the rest she needs.

You'll also appreciate the quiet time. Perhaps you can

nap at the same time. If you're feeling impatient with your child, a nap for each of you may be the best approach.

No Mealtime Arguments

We all like mealtime to be pleasant. Mealtime arguments can spoil everyone's appetite. Now is the time, while your child is small, to start the habit of happy mealtimes. Fussing at your child to get him to eat will get you nowhere.

Most toddlers gain only three to five pounds between 12 and 24 months, and another three to five pounds by age 3. It's important for you to understand this slower growth rate because this means your toddler may not need to eat as much as you think he should.

Toddlers may go through stages when they will eat only a few foods. It's okay to have a limited diet as long as it's balanced. Try to have something from each of the Food Pyramid food groups each day. His diet may seem monotonous to you, but that's all right.

Children who are served nutritious food and very little junk food tend to eat when they're hungry. If they aren't hungry, they probably shouldn't eat anyway. So don't nag! Instead, use mealtime to talk about what's happening today.

If it's just you and your child, you can talk about the shape and color of the food, how it was prepared, where milk comes from, and other topics of interest to your child. If other family members are present, conversation won't be so child-centered, but it can still be concerned mostly with the pleasant happenings of the day.

"Where Do Babies Come From?"

Your toddler may start asking questions about sex. If he does, let him know you appreciate his questions, then answer in terms he can understand. When he asks, " Where do babies come from?" you might say, " Babies grow in a special place in the mother's body."

If he asks how the baby got inside the mother, you can tell him that a mother and a father make a baby together. You might explain that the father's sperm gets into the mother through the father's penis.

Sometimes little girls worry because they have no penis, and little boys worry that their penis might come off. Explain that boys and girls are made differently. Teach your child the correct names for his/her genitals. Name them as you name other body parts.

All little boys and girls handle their genitals. When they do, and find that this feels good, they may masturbate. This does no harm. It is normal, and you would be wise to ignore it. A parent who tells his/her child that masturbation is bad may cause the child to feel naughty, or to think that sex or sexual feelings are bad. That's not a very realistic or healthy approach.

Potty Training (Teaching)

He's 30 months old now. Toilet training is one thing that's very difficult right now. He loves wearing training pants, and he says he's a big boy then.

He knows why he has to go in the toilet, but he's scared when he has to do #2. For about two days he went pretty good. He'd try so hard, but sometimes he'd start crying. I'd leave him there, and he'd come running and pee on the carpet.

Sometimes he goes into the bathroom, and he will say, " Take my diapers down." He will pee with his dad, but he's not ready for #2. Sometimes on the weekends I let him wear his underwear, and he will tell everybody. But if he has to go pee, he will wet his pants.

Jessica, 17 - Craig, 2½

This little boy is showing many signs of stress, and his parents are, too. He wants to succeed and please his parents, but developmentally he's not quite ready. It would be better to wait a month or two, then try teaching again. By then he may have developed the ability to hold his urine or release it when he chooses. He may be more able to control his bowel movement (BM), too.

Little boys often learn later than little girls. Many are unable to learn until they're three or even older. It's a lot less stressful and more productive not to try teaching him to go to the toilet until he's developmentally ready.

Often a child will like to use the potty at first. He may enjoy the new training pants or potty chair, but the added attention he's getting probably is more important to him. He may lose interest as toileting settles into a routine. Putting him back in diapers, and trying again a month or so later is a good idea.

If you can be relaxed about toilet teaching, it will be much easier for everyone. For a broader discussion of this topic, see *Discipline from Birth to Three*.

Hard to Accept Change

The last couple of days Ellie wants me all the time. She wants to be with me 24 hours a day. Her father left two months ago, and she's happier now, but I think that made her feel a little insecure.

Shalimar

Ellie may be " happier now" that her father is gone, but at the same time, she undoubtedly misses him. She needs some extra attention from her mother for awhile. For all kinds of reasons, your child may become more dependent on you at about age two, especially if you have to be separated from him for awhile. It's hard for children of this

"You can't see me." (Her version of hide and seek.)

age to cope with change in their lives. If you must leave
your child with a new babysitter, let him have time to
adjust to the person before you leave. A big change like dad
leaving or even the family moving into a different home
may be especially difficult for your toddler.

If you're moving, prepare in advance. Talk to your child
about it. As you pack, let him pack some of his toys in a
box. You may need to repack them later, but if you let him
be a part of the process, it will all seem less strange to him.

Tell him how the furniture and clothing, and especially
his toys, will be moved from one place to the other. Explain
what your new home will be like, and where he will sleep
and play. Let him see it in advance if possible. The more
familiar the moving process is to him, the less anxious he is
likely to be.

Toddlers are more secure when their life has a predictable routine. They want to sleep in their own bed with a special blanket or stuffed animal. Mom or dad may be the only ones who can put them to bed without tears. The same may be true of eating. They want a predictable routine.

Even More Patience Needed

While your two-year-old may appear clingy and dependent at times, at other times she will insist on doing things her way:

If she sets her mind on something, she'll do it whether I want her to or not. If I want to do her hair, she won't let me do it. She gets in these moods where she won't let anybody touch her. In fact, sometimes she kicks and she screams over almost nothing.

Shalimar

This can be a difficult time for a toddler. She wants so much to be independent, but simply can't do everything she wants to do. It's best to allow time for her to dress and undress herself, and to be available when she can't quite do it alone. At times she will be cooperative, and at other times, extremely unreasonable. Develop your patience to the fullest. This is not the time to allow yourself the luxury of being impatient. Your toddler needs your help to cope with her moodiness.

He doesn't listen to us. He always likes to do his own thing, and he's demanding. He says "No" to everything, and he always asks "Why?"

Sarah, 17 - Leon, 2½

Now you need to be especially consistent in your interactions with your child. If you tell her one thing today, you need to follow the same rule tomorrow.

Routine is important for two-year-olds. She likes to do

things the same way day after day after day. Her bedtime routine may become even more elaborate.

These are busy months for you and for your toddler. She still has much to learn about her world. If she's given plenty of opportunity to explore, as we've said so often in these books, she'll learn more. She also will keep you alert as you supervise her exploring!

People say she's spoiled, but I don't let her go too far. She's a kid, and they explore and they do things. If you put too many limitations on a child, you never know how much she can learn.

Shalimar

Winning — For Both of You

Talking about a power struggle between a grown-up (you) and your toddler may sound silly. Of course you have the power if we're talking about physical force. If your child won't go to bed, you can pick her up, even if she's kicking and screaming, and put her in her bed.

If you do this, who wins? Certainly not your child. And you don't win either if she's crying and screaming and extremely unhappy.

Try to get inside your toddler's head for a minute. How does she feel? At the same time, think about how you feel. What can you do so you *both* will win?

Time may be a big factor in this kind of stress. You have a great deal to do. If you're in school and/or have a job, you need to get a lot done while you're with your child. It's normal to try to hurry her at mealtime, when she's getting dressed, and when it's time for her to go to bed. As she feels pressured, however, she's likely to dawdle even more. Perhaps she'll declare flatly that she's not going to eat, or go to bed, or get dressed, or whatever it is she must do.

Experiment with taking ten more minutes to get her ready for school. Stretch that bedtime routine a little more. You may find she's more likely to go along with what you want her to do.

Setting a timer might help. For example, show her a timer set for ten minutes. Explain that when the timer dings, lunch will be ready. Toddlers tend to be completely absorbed in their play and dislike being interrupted. They need closure. Advance notice that it's almost time to change activities may help her cooperate.

You're His Model

I think it's very very hard being a parent. I don't regret it, but I wish I had waited. Seeing Johnnie grow up as a little person is making me think twice before I act because he mimics me and looks up to me.

I'm the person he copies, his role model. I used to dip cookies in my milk and Johnnie started doing that. My boyfriend said, " If you don't want your son to do that, you can't do it." He was right, of course.

Natalie

Being your child's role model is an awesome responsibility. Observe your child playing with dolls and you're likely to learn how you sound to him. Children whose parents yell a lot often yell at their dolls. It is also true that children whose parents take the time to explain their activities to their child may find him talking in a similar fashion with his "baby."

Toddlers need a lot of attention. They're growing and learning rapidly. Positive attention from significant persons makes the learning seem more meaningful and important.

Watching him learn is exciting for you. Experiencing that learning is even more exciting for your toddler.

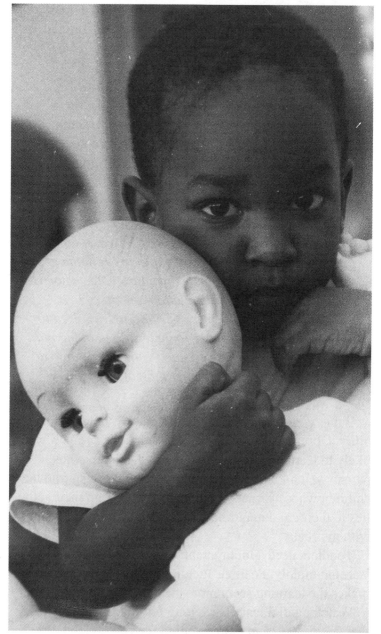

Many two-year-olds enjoy playing with dolls.

9

Playing with Your Two-Year-Old

- **Sometimes She's Self-Sufficient**
- **Home-Made Toys**
- **Time for Finger Painting**
- **Teaching with Games**
- **Helping Mom and Dad**
- **Celebrating Holidays**
- **How Much TV?**
- **Select Programs Carefully**
- **Playing Outside**
- **Cold Weather OK?**
- **An Athlete Already?**

Skye plays real good by herself. She puts the rope and the beads together.

She makes believe a lot. She flies children around the room and tells me she's flying all over the house. Yesterday she told me she made a choo-choo train.

When I go to softball practice, Skye and her dad pick me up afterward. She'll say, "Mommy, I play softball?"

I say, "Not until you're bigger."

She'll say, "Okay."

Or she'll say, "I go to school, Mommy, I go to school?" I tell her not yet. Or when I'm doing

*my homework, she puts her colors in her backpack
and tells me she's going to school, and she's doing
her homework.*

*We listen to sing along tapes, and Skye loves to
sing and she likes to dance. Every time a song comes
on that she likes, she'll say, "Mom, let's dance!"*

Molly, 18 - Skye, 33 months

Sometimes She's Self-Sufficient

Your two-year-old is more self-sufficient now. She can
play by herself, but she still loves and needs your attention.
If you play with her regularly, she will learn more. She'll
also be more willing to play by herself other times.

This doesn't mean you need to spend all your time
entertaining her. That wouldn't be good for her either.
Some of the time she'll be satisfied to play near you while
you do your work.

Made-at-Home Toys

Even if he owns a lot of toys, your toddler is likely to
prefer homemade items much of the time. One of the best
toys you can give him is a big box. If you or someone you
know buys a new TV or, even better, a refrigerator or other
big appliance, save the box.

Your toddler will love going in and out of it. Together
you can cut windows and doors in his new house. He can
decorate it with crayons or paints. He can pretend it's his
home one day, a school house the next. He can hide from
you in his house. You'll hear him giggling as you look
for him.

He can use a smaller box for a cook stove. Turn the box
over and help your toddler draw burners on the bottom.
Help him "cook" a snack for the two of you, then "eat"
with him.

Larissa loves Winnie the Pooh. She has a Pooh Bear, and she puts him in his little crib and tells him "Night-night." She rocks his little crib and pretends like she's putting him to sleep.

She has little fake baby food, and she feeds him. On the weekends she'll pretend like the school bus is outside. She'll go over to her bear and say, "The bus is coming. I have to go now."

Leila, 18 - Larissa, 2½

Encourage him in his pretend play. He may have an imaginary friend. He may even talk to his friend. Imaginary play is a healthy part of growing up.

Do you have a card table you can set up near you? Drape a sheet or blanket over it, and your toddler has a tent or a cave or whatever he wishes. Let his imagination take over.

When you're cleaning out your closets, choose some cast-offs for a dress-up box for your child. He'll like old hats, scarves, mom's or dad's shoes, and other grown-up clothing. Include costume jewelry that's safe for your child, things he can't swallow. Encourage your toddler to pretend he's someone else as he dresses up.

Time for Finger Painting

Let him finger paint. Of course he'll taste and examine the paint first. Then he may paint a little.

Recipe

You can make a safe (from a tasting standpoint — it still makes a mess!) finger paint by mixing two table-spoons of cornstarch into two tablespoons of cold water. Then add one cup boiling water and stir again.

For color, use food coloring . Or use one tablespoon of yellow prepared mustard to two tablespoons of the base to make a canary yellow paint.

Finger painting takes some preparation. Put old clothes on your child and lots of newspapers on the floor. A small chair and table with lots of working space would be ideal, but a high chair will do.

Almost any kind of plain paper is all right for finger painting — brown wrapping paper, paper bags, cardboard from shirt and panty hose packages. Tape the paper to the table or tray before he starts painting. Or you could let him finger paint in the bath tub — with supervision, of course.

After all this preparation, he may do more tasting than painting. Show him how to use the paint on the paper. He may find the whole thing a bit weird, but he'll probably have a ball. He'll enjoy it even more if you paint with him.

Take a tip from preschool teachers and do a little organizing of your child's day. Plan a time when she can finger paint or paint with a brush. If the weather permits, painting outside cuts back on cleanup time. Provide plenty of opportunities for your toddler to color, paint, cut paper (with blunt-ended scissors), and other creative activities. You'll continue to supervise, of course:

> *In my house the crayons are up in the closet where Mickey can't reach. It's special when he can color, or paint, or cut paper. If he wants to cut 100 pieces of paper, that's fine, but he must do it in a special place.*
> Susan, 20 - Mickey, 2 1/2; Felicia, 11 months

She's not ready to color or paint between the lines in a coloring book. In fact, if she's at all creative, she won't "be ready" later either. Coloring books are a poor investment. Giving her big pieces of paper, then encouraging her to draw or scribble as she thinks best is a far better approach.

> *Luke likes to write a lot. I open big paper bags and turn the blank side out. I tape it on the wall, and it's like a big chalkboard. He writes all over it. That keeps*

him busy for a long time. Of course I have to watch
that he stays on the paper.

Ashley, 18 - Luke, 34 months; Abby, 20 months

Don't worry whether your child uses her left or her right
hand. Children often appear to change handedness several
times before settling into using one or the other as their
"working" hand. Whichever hand she uses is okay. The
important thing is not to try to change her preference.

If she's left-handed, she's part of the 15 percent of the
population with this preference. By her third birthday, you
probably can tell whether she's right or left handed.

Teaching with Games

You can teach your child colors by talking about the
color of his clothes and of other things around him. You
can make games by coloring circles of paper various bright
colors. Then draw the same size circles on a sheet of paper
and color those circles to match the others. Can he match
the red cut-out circle with the red circle on the paper?

Does your toddler know his name? If he is separated
from you, can he tell someone who he is? You can help
him learn by making it a game. Ask him to name family
members in photographs, and include photos of him.

Doll play is important to many two-year-olds. If you
nave another baby now, your toddler may be especially
interested in his own baby.

Haley has a friend who comes over a lot. They play
in the playhouse with their dolls. They change them
and talk to them.

She'll say, "We're going bye-bye. We have to get
ready for school," like I do every morning. One time I
heard her say, "Oh-h-h, I'll tell grandma on you."

Bettiann, 20 - Haley, 35 months

Helping Mom and Dad

Pretend play for a two-year-old often means imitating mom or dad.

Ricardo wants to do everything I do. When he sees me cooking, he wants to cook. When his dad says he's hungry, Ricardo runs to the kitchen and wants to fix him something. I let him bring the food to his daddy, and he feels great.

Sometimes when I'm washing the dishes Ricardo wants to help me. I say, "Ricardo, come here and help me," and he comes running in. He brings his chair over to the sink, and I let him rinse the dishes.

Sharon, 19 - Ricardo, 35 months; Monique, 16 months

By the time your child is three years old, he'll be able to

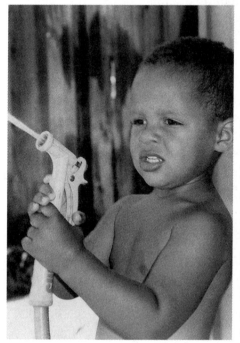

He's watering the yard.

"help" you in many ways. He can set the table, especially if you provide lightweight plastic dishes. He can help make his own snack by putting some grated cheese on a tortilla, folding over the tortilla, and heating it, with your help, either in the microwave or the regular oven. He can help carry in the groceries. He can dust furniture, although you want to be careful about giving him a treated dust cloth because you don't want him to put it in his mouth. He'd love to "work" with a feather duster. He can help pick up trash. In fact, he may be willing to help you do all sorts of things.

For most children of this age, the magic word is *help*. He probably won't be willing to take on all these jobs simply because you ask him to. His incentive in doing jobs is to be like you.

Celebrating Holidays

Donovan saw Santa, and he was scared. We went to the mall, and he didn't like Santa much. That was okay. We didn't have to take a picture. We were in line, and he saw the little kids going to Santa. He said, "No, I don't want it." So we left, and everything was fine.

Belia, 17 - Donovan, 2

Dalton loves Halloween and Christmas, but Santa, he doesn't like. He's not too sure of the big fat guy in red.

Claire, 17 - Dalton, 33 months

You may be eager to share Halloween with your child. Or you may be looking forward to introducing your toddler to Santa Claus at your local department store. You may find, however, that your little one is not thrilled with either experience.

Santa Claus may scare your toddler because she thinks he's real. He's big and fat, he wears funny clothes, has a peculiar beard, and he sits there and glares at her. She may burst into tears and ruin your photograph.

Halloween scares many toddlers for the same reason. They don't understand fantasy, and they believe these outlandish characters are real.

To help make these events less frightening, talk to your toddler beforehand about where you're going and what you'll see. Maybe you can practice. Show her pictures of Santa. Play with masks together before Halloween.

When the day arrives, don't rush your child into this new experience. Let her watch other children climbing on Santa's lap. Don't pressure her to follow their lead. She may decide it's okay, or she may not. If she doesn't want to see Santa this year, respect her feelings. Perhaps she'll be ready next year.

On Halloween, she might like to hand out candy to the trick or treaters while you hold her.

How Much Television?

People shouldn't use TV as a babysitter. It rots their brain, and they don't have an interest in reading. Sergy and Leonardo have a lot of books, and I tell them to read or play with their toys instead of settling for television.

I let them watch two shows, and that's a whole hour. At this age, that's enough. My best friend lets her son watch videos all day. We'd rather go to the park instead.

Kerrianne, 19 - Sergy, 3; Leonardo, 4

In many families, television viewing is a fact of life. The set will be tuned into a variety of programs throughout the day and evening. If you're in your parents' home, you may not have much control over television viewing.

Television probably does more to prevent learning for children under three than it teaches them. This is true even when the programs are carefully selected and limited to those which are supposed to be appropriate for the young child.

Your child needs to interact actively with his environment to learn about it. He needs to smell, taste, feel, and handle objects with his hands to discover what they're like and what he can do with them. Just looking and listening isn't enough.

Unfamiliar objects seen on the screen have little or no meaning. He may not even recognize familiar objects. Yet without guidance, a child may appear to be content in front of the TV screen:

> *Alina will sit in a chair and watch TV for hours if she has her pillow, and she can hold it and suck her thumb.*
>
> Joanne, 23 - Francene, 4; Alina, 3; Gloria, 1

Alina, like all children, needs to run, crawl, jump, roll, and climb. Children enjoy doing these things with other children because they're beginning to learn social skills. These skills need to be actively practiced. That doesn't happen in front of the TV.

Although a child may hear many words spoken on television, watching too much TV is likely to delay her language development. If she's absorbed in the TV, she isn't talking, and learning to talk takes lots of practice. If she does try to speak, no one is there to answer. She needs to talk to someone who will respond to her.

Select Programs Carefully

> *We don't want Elena watching horror films. In fact, I don't think a child should watch that much TV. It's not good for their development. There's too much violence, and it can pollute their minds.*
>
> Raul, 19 - Elena, 23 months

When your child watches TV, you need to select her programs carefully. So much of television has strong

emotional situations which are upsetting to children. It's
not real, it gives a distorted view of violence, a distorted
view of sex, and has enormous emotional overload for
your child.

Programs showing violent behavior and angry people
may be quite disturbing to her. She may not fully understand what she sees, and her ability to use words is too
limited for her to be able to talk about it.

If other people are interested in watching the program,
they may even tell your child to be quiet. They may dis-
courage the few questions she might have tried to ask.

Any program your child watches should be suitable for
his age, and it should be viewed with someone who will
talk to him about it. Ideally, children under three should not
watch TV for more than an hour each day.

If you live in a home where the television is on regularly
for long hours, try to keep your child away from the set and
its noise. You can rescue the kids — put them in a separate
room with toys away from the TV.

If you watch a lot of TV, your child may follow your
example and miss out on the active play she needs. Or she
may take advantage of your involvement with television
and get into trouble:

> *When I get stuck on the TV, it's as if they say,*
> *"Forget it." They go off and do things I don't let them*
> *do. When I don't pay any attention to them, they get*
> *into all kinds of things.*
>
> Joanne

Even if you enjoy watching TV, you may decide to
sacrifice some of your shows to spend time with your child.
You're a far better teacher than the television can ever be.
Let her have the advantage of your companionship rather
than letting the TV set become her companion.

Research shows that aggressive children tend to watch a lot of violence on television. Research also shows that children who watch too much TV show less imagination in their play and at school than do children who watch less television.

A toddler who sits in front of the TV set for several hours each day is not involved in the active play he needs. He's also undoubtedly watching shows inappropriate for him — shows with scary scenes, shows which give a distorted view of relationships between men and women, and other situations which tend to scare or confuse him. Even the evening news often includes frightening coverage of the day's violence.

Children can learn important things from television, however. Can you watch TV with your child and talk with him about what he sees and hears? If the two of you watch an hour of carefully selected shows a day, and talk together about it, TV may have a positive influence on your toddler.

If your family watches a lot of TV, you may have little choice in the number of hours the set is on each day. Probably the best tactic in this case is to find a quiet place where you and your child can play away from TV.

Playing Outside

If it's nice, we play outside, or we go to the park. I name everything, the leaves and the sky, and talk about the colors.

Molly

Playing outside is important to two-year-olds. If you're lucky enough to have a fenced-in yard, she'll probably spend hours there, especially if you can be with her. Remember that she still needs lots of supervision. If your yard is not securely fenced, you'll need to be with her constantly

She's practicing her balancing skills at the park.

when she's outside.

Toddlers love to play in sand, dirt, and mud. Give him spoons, cups, and other sand toys. It's best to keep a sandbox covered when he's not playing in it. This keeps out the cats and dogs who like sand, too.

He can paint the garage or outside wall if you get him a small bucket of water and a paint brush. He'll love playing with a squirt bottle filled with water. By now he may be able to blow soap bubbles.

If you don't have a yard, can you take him to a nearby park often? Taking him for a walk each day will satisfy some of his need to be outside. Of course this won't be the kind of walk where you get lots of exercise from walking rapidly. Your toddler will explore all sorts of things along the way. He'll be in no hurry.

Outings to the airport to watch the planes landing and taking off, to the train station, and to a building site will excite him as much as taking him to Disneyland. Of course, if you're observing a construction site, you and your child will hold hands as you watch.

We stop for fire engines. We go to the harbor and watch the boats. Haley points at helicopters going over and says, "Copters."
We take her to a petting farm where there are chickens and goats. Haley likes to pet them. We started going there when she was 2.
We also go to the park and feed the ducks.

Bettiann

If you live near a beach, you and your toddler may enjoy playing there. Of course you'll be constantly watching her. You also need to be extra careful about sunburn. Most toddlers have sensitive skin and burn easily.

She loves the beach. When the waves go out, she runs down there, then runs back when they're coming in. She likes chasing the birds, and she loves to lie in the sand.

Shalimar, 19 - Ellie, 2 1/2

What About Cold Weather?

Toddlers enjoy playing outside. It's good for them. They are usually more active outside than inside. The exercise helps their motor development. It also gives them a better appetite and makes them more ready for bedtime.

But what about cold weather? Claire doesn't much like the cold, so Mitch plays in the snow with Dalton:

Dalton and his dad make snowmen, and they have little snowball fights. I'm not big on cold weather, but I usually watch from the window with a cup of hot chocolate.

Claire

On the other hand, Cathi says:

Susie loves to go outside but it's cold already. She has to be inside a lot or she'll get sick. We try to explain, but she's still too little to understand.

Cathi, 18 - Susie, 34 months

This sounds like a power struggle. Cold temperatures don't make babies sick. Germs do. Usually a preschool child can be bundled up warm enough not to get cold when she's playing outside. Susie is probably quite active while she's playing and may not feel cold at all.

The mother may have a much bigger problem trying to stay warm. Cathi may not be dressed as warmly, and she is undoubtedly less active than her child.

The mother should claim the problem. She should tell her daughter that she's cold and needs to go back in the house now to get warm. Together they could work on some rules for outside play such as the length of time they'll stay outside. It might help if an indoor play area with room for active play could be arranged for days when she really can't go outside.

An Athlete Already?

I think Luke's going to be a good baseball player. His dad likes to play baseball with him. When we play, Luke knows how to hold his little plastic bat real good. He hits the ball a lot when we throw it at him.

Ashley

Lots of fathers and mothers look forward to playing ball with their children. By the time she's two, dad may be playing catch with her. She's not ready for rules yet, but she may thoroughly enjoy playing ball her way with mom or dad.

Leon's parents described his ball-playing mania:

Jordan: Leon watches basketball with me. He knows how to dribble a basketball already. He doesn't like to play with trucks, but he plays with balls constantly.

Sarah: When I tell him to throw his clothes in the hamper, he shoots them in, and yells, "Two points!" He watches sports on TV all the time with his dad.

Rough-housing is an activity that toddlers and parents, especially dads, often enjoy. It's not smart, however, to play at hitting each other if you don't want your child to hit other children. Neither is it wise to get your child so excited that he'll have trouble calming down.

I think parents set the pace. My husband likes to play rough. Then he gets tired and wants to stop, but the kids aren't ready to stop. You can't just all of a sudden stop. You have to start going slower and taking it easier. It took him awhile to learn that.

Annabel, 27 - Andrew, 10; Anthony, 7; Bianca, 5; James, 2

Active play usually is not a good idea at bedtime. You want your child to slow down. That's why a bedtime routine including a storytime works best.

The whole world is fantastic to your toddler. Everything is new. Toddlers really don't need Disneyland because they can find excitement wherever they are. Your job is to share his excitement, and to guide and support him as he discovers his world. *Have fun!*

She needs to hold your hand when she crosses the street.

10

Guarding Your Toddler's Health and Safety

- **Toddler Needs Even More Supervision**
- **Protect Him from Burns**
- **Cars Can Be Deadly**
- **Preventing Serious Illness**
- **Your Baby Needs a Doctor**
- **Diarrhea Is Still Dangerous**
- **When Your Child Gets Sick**
- **Ear Infections Must Be Treated**
- **Caring for Toddlers' Teeth**

Kamie slides the chair over, and gets up on the counter. She's been standing on the top part of the couch, the back of it. Last night she was jumping off the couch. She fell off and sprained her ankle, but by today she was ready to jump off the couch again. I told her, "No more."

I put away the stuff that would be dangerous, including moving plants up to a higher cabinet she couldn't reach. I didn't want anything to happen to her.

Lucas, 21 - Kamie, 21 months

Tatiana has had a fever several times, and one time she broke out in hives. I put cortisone on her

and left her uncovered for a little while so her fever
could drop. The hives went away the next day.
*   She gets sick quite often, I think because she just*
started a new day care. She gets sick real easy, so
either my mom has to take off or I have to stay home
from school to take care of her.

Mihaela, 16 - Tatiana, 18 months

Your Toddler Needs Even More Supervision

*   We're in an apartment, and sometimes there's*
broken glass on the sidewalk. I pick it up when I see
it, but I can't get it all.
*   Luke and Abby like to go barefoot outside. Once*
Luke stepped on some glass and cut his foot, so now
he wears shoes. In hot weather he likes sandals.

Ashley, 18 - Luke, 34 months; Abby, 20 months

You probably were quite safety conscious during your
child's first year. You didn't leave him alone even for a
minute on a bed or changing table even though you "knew"
he couldn't turn over. You realized how quickly a baby can
roll off such a surface.

When your baby started crawling, you may have
checked out your home at his eye level. This is a good way
to spot the dangers. You probably covered the electric
outlets, and perhaps you were able to child-proof your
home to a great extent.

Your toddler needs even more careful watching than he
did a few months earlier. He's running everywhere, but his
judgment develops much more slowly. During this sensory
motor stage, the steady supervision must continue. He has
to try things to find out what will happen, yet he's unable to
think it through and predict what will really happen. It's
your job to keep him safe.

Don't ever leave your baby or toddler alone in your

house or apartment, even if he's sleeping. Don't ever leave him alone in your parked car either, even if you're just running into the store for one quick item.

Children left in cars in the summer can die from the heat. Closed cars get much hotter than the outside air, somewhat like an oven. There is also the danger the child will lock the doors and not be able to get out in an emergency.

He can probably turn doorknobs and open doors by his second birthday. It's even more important that you keep dangerous things out of his sight and out of his reach. It's doubly important to keep trash cans securely covered or in a closed-off area when toddlers are running around. A small child can get in lots of trouble by playing in the trash.

Check your home again for hazards. Many almost-toddlers climb amazingly well even before they walk. Climbing means she can get into even more trouble if you don't watch her constantly.

He doesn't know. The whole world is a big adventure, and that's scary. He could fall on something, and he always wants to put things in his mouth. It takes 24 hours of supervision — unless he's sleeping. Then you can finally relax.

My grandpa does a lot of watching because when I was little, I almost died when I choked on an apple. He's there watching, watching, being protective. Nathan is really quick and, when he's outside, he can run out in the street so fast.

Esteban, 18 - Nathan, 2; Ralph, 5 months

Protect Him from Burns

One day I left my curling iron on the bathroom counter. I had turned it off, but it was still hot. Haley went into the bathroom and put her hand on it. She

started screaming, "I touched hot. I touched hot."
It made a blister, and I put ice on it. The doctor
said not to pop the blister, so I didn't.

                                        Bettiann, 20 - Haley, 35 months

Toddlers are at great risk for being burned. They can be
scalded by pulling a cup of coffee or tea off the table onto
themselves. They can be burned by touching a hot stove,
iron, or heater. When you're carrying hot food to the table,
you must be extremely careful. If your toddler is playing on
the floor beside you, you could spill hot food on him.

When he's learning to walk, his ability to reach develops
rapidly. The child who was confined to crawling on the
floor last week may be pulling himself up by grabbing the
table or the stove this week. Hot food, liquids, and heavy
items must *not* be left near the edge of the table or stove.

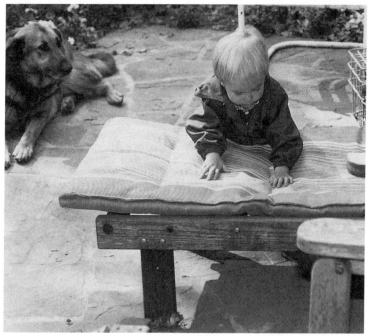

Make sure the things he can climb are safe for him.

Poisoning Is Big Danger

One time I left a cup of bleach up on the sink. I guess Luke thought it was water and he drank it. I smelled something and I realized the smell came from his mouth. I ran to get my mother. By the time we got back, my husband had put his finger down Luke's throat and made him throw up.

Now we don't leave anything like that lying around. We're also careful about small objects because the kids could choke on them.

Ashley

Children are most likely to be poisoned when they're ten to twenty months old. They move around a lot, explore everything in reach, put everything possible in their mouths, and aren't able to understand what's dangerous and what's not. They also will drink things that taste terrible (to us).

Cigarettes are poisonous. If members of your family smoke, use your best negotiating skills to get them to help keep ash trays out of the reach of your toddler.

The fact that your toddler goes everywhere and explores everything is exciting because you know that's how he's learning. It's also scary because you know how easily he can be hurt. If it's a white powder, he thinks it's sugar. If it's a colored liquid, it must be juice. It may actually be a poisonous perfume or insecticide, but he probably won't know the difference.

It's your job to keep your child safe. Check your house, garage and yard often for items that could be dangerous to touch or eat.

Know the plants around your home. Oleander and castor beans, for example, are dangerous if eaten, and can kill a child.

Find the telephone number of your nearest Poison Control Center. Keep it by your phone along with your doctor's and other emergency numbers. If you think your child has been poisoned, take any evidence you have of what he swallowed, a piece of the substance or the container it was in.

Get some syrup of ipecac from your pharmacist and use it if your doctor or poison control center recommends it. It will help your child throw up. For some poisons, this is appropriate. For others, such as toilet and drain cleaners, it's exactly what you *don't* want. Throwing up Drano will cause twice the damage because the lye burns going down and again coming up.

Cars Can Be Deadly

When William gets in the car, the first thing he does is fasten his seat belt. He's used to it. If I don't fasten mine instantly, he says, "You don't have yours on."

I say, "Okay," and I put it on.

Ruthie Faye, 19 - William, 4; Soraya, 18 months

Cars can be deadly for toddlers. If he's in the car, make sure he's buckled into his car seat. If he weighs 40 pounds or more, he can use the regular seat belt. Incidentally, be just as sure that you're buckled in, too. You're his model.

Going in the street — that's a big one. Right away she thinks she can go in the street. One day she ran out, and here comes a car. I screamed at her and spanked her. Since then, she goes up to the curb, she looks, and then she walks away.

I say, "If the ball goes in the street, you come get Mommy," and "If your friends cross the street, don't follow them. You come to me and I'll help you."

*We cross the street together. She's learning. I tell
her all the time, "Cars won't see you, Haley," and
she'll say, "Okay, Mommy, I'll wait for you."*

Bettiann

Your toddler moves quickly, but is only now beginning
to develop the ability and self-control to stay out of busy
streets and to watch for cars as he crosses even a garage
driveway. Insist that he hold your hand when you cross a
street, go through a parking lot, or across a driveway.

For a more detailed discussion of making your home
safe for your toddler, see *Your Baby's First Year.*

Preventing Serious Illness

Your child should see your healthcare provider for a
checkup about every nine to twelve months during his
second and third years. Before you go to the doctor, write
down your questions. It's easy to forget them when you're
face to face with your super-busy doctor.

You've probably made sure your toddler got his twelve
immunizations on schedule during his first year. When he's
18 months old, he needs to go back for "refills."

A new vaccine called Rv (Rotavirus) was recently
introduced. It prevents diarrhea, and is generally given
during the first year.

At 12-15 months she'll need to be immunized against
rubella (German measles), mumps, and red measles
(MMR). She should also have a skin test for tuberculosis at
that time. Your healthcare provider may also recommend
she receive the chickenpox (varicella) vaccine sometime
during his second year.

Your Baby Needs a Doctor

*Celeste and Carrie have gotten real sick this
winter. We've been to the doctor like ten times. I don't*

take them outside, I give them vitamins, but one gets
sick, and then the other one.
    What do I do when they get sick? I call my
grandma. If she can't help, I take them to the doctor
and get medicine. When they're sick, they sleep quite
a bit, but they both want to be held together. It's
real hard.

                    Noelle-Marie, 19 - Celeste, 21/2; Carrie, 9 months

If you don't have a healthcare provider for your child,
call your local health department. They will give you
the name of a doctor and/or tell you of a health department
clinic where your child can get a health examination.

   Should you have any questions regarding your child's
health, be sure to check with your healthcare provider.
Write down your observations in advance. They may help
your doctor make a diagnosis.

   Regular checkups are a good time to ask questions about
your child's health and about his growth and development.
Talk with your healthcare provider about caring for a sick
child at home. Ask what to give for a fever.

   How high should your child's temperature be before you
call the doctor? Is there a cough syrup to keep on hand?
How about allergy medicines?

   Your child's vision and hearing will be checked as part
of his well-baby examination. Any other examinations by
specialists should be done only if recommended by your
healthcare provider.

Diarrhea Still Dangerous

   When your child was an infant, you knew how dangerous diarrhea could be. You probably called your doctor
soon after the diarrhea started because you didn't want your
baby to become dehydrated. Diarrhea is still a dangerous

condition for your child. Because it causes dehydration, diarrhea can be a very serious problem for toddlers, too.

The two most important things in caring for the child with diarrhea are:

- Give lots of liquids.
- Give little or no fat-containing foods such as French fries or butter.

When Your Child Gets Sick

Haley got strep throat once when I did. She was about 14 months old, and I was trying to take care of her by myself. My mom and dad were gone on vacation, and I was scared and didn't know what to do. She was feverish, and I kept her in the bathtub for a long time.

Then my aunt came over and said, "You're going to the doctor." She took us both in, and he prescribed antibiotics for both of us. That was a terrible week.

Bettiann

Eating a popsicle helps provide the liquid she needs if she has a fever or is nauseous.

Doctors often give antibiotics

such as penicillin. It is *very* important to give *all* of the medicine to your child so the illness doesn't return in a week or two. Sometimes moms think they can save some medicine to use the next time the child is sick. This is not smart.

If not all the germs are killed, those that remain are likely to become resistant to the antibiotic. Next time your child has a similar illness, the antibiotic may not work. To repeat, give your child *all* the medicine prescribed.

Colds are difficult in the preschool years. Attending school is usually a nice experience for the child but unfortunately, she is likely to get one or two more colds. The first year the child attends any school, this is likely to happen. If the parent waits until she's ready for kindergarten, it will probably happen then.

He had a cough when I took him in for his checkup. The doctor said to put the vaporizer on at night, and that seems to help. He's getting better.

Evangelina, 18 - Ricardo, 3 1/2; Raul, 27 months

A cold-water vaporizer is a good investment. Using it in your child's room will help him breathe more easily when he's congested. Some children have a particularly rough time with asthma and/or allergies:

Luke gets sick often, mostly coughs and congestion. I think it's allergies. The doctor said it may develop into asthma. They have to give him antibiotics.

He got a real high fever once, and I put him in the bathtub with cool water. He was crying, but my mom was there to help me.

Ashley

Having *their* mother's help when their child is sick is very reassuring for many young parents.

Ear Infections Must Be Treated

Abby had an ear infection last week. I could tell because she's usually a real active baby, but she only wanted to sit on my lap.

She was pulling at her ear, and I said, "Abby, does your ear hurt?" She nodded. Of course I took her to the doctor.

Ashley

If your child appears to have an ear infection, *call the doctor.* Untreated ear infections, in addition to being quite painful, can easily cause loss of hearing. A child who can't hear well misses out on a lot, and is likely to have a difficult time when he starts school.

If he can't hear, he will have a hard time learning to talk. He won't hear how words should sound. His language will sound garbled and be hard to understand.

Most ear infections, if caught soon enough, can be treated with no lasting problem.

Ellie had a lot of ear infections that first year. Then we realized she wasn't talking, and our friends' babies were talking a lot. We took her to an ear, nose and throat doctor, and he said, "She can't hear."

We sat in a room where a little monkey rang a bell. Ellie wouldn't even look when he rang the bell.

I felt so bad when I found out she was deaf. We had yelled at her, "Ellie, come here," and she wouldn't respond. Then we'd get mad at her.

They did surgery on her ears, and she's hearing fine now. Two days after the surgery I said, "Ellie," and she looked at me. A couple of days later she was saying "Mommy" for the first time. She also likes music now. She couldn't hear it before.

Shalimar, 19 - Ellie, 30 months

For a more detailed discussion on your child's health care, see *Your Baby's First Year.*

Caring for Toddler's Teeth

Your toddler may have had no trouble cutting his early teeth. His first and second molars, which come through during his second year, can be a different matter. He may be quite miserable and irritable when these molars are coming through his gums.

Some things you can do to help include giving him something cold to bite on, using a teething cream, or giving a pain medication (such as Tylenol) when he's miserable. He may like to play with ice cubes. Even rubbing his gums with your finger may help, if only to let him know you're trying to do something for him.

It's important to take good care of his baby teeth.

If he seems to be in a lot of pain, it may not be his teeth. If he keeps putting his hand up to the side of his face, perhaps he has an earache. Check with his doctor.

Your toddler needs his own toothbrush. You should be brushing his teeth as soon as three or four teeth have erupted. Now he will want to help, but be sure his teeth are brushed thoroughly at least twice a day.

The easiest way to show him how to brush is to stand him in front of you with the back of his head against you. Brace his head against one hand and brush with the other. Show him how to brush the upper teeth down and the lower teeth up, the way they grow. You'll need to supervise his brushing for several years yet.

Those baby teeth have three important uses:

- They help him move from only milk to solid foods he can chew.
- Baby teeth help shape the child's jaw.
- They help him pronounce words correctly.

For these reasons, you need to take your toddler in for a dental checkup by age 3. If there are cavities, it's important to have them filled.

Keeping your child safe and healthy during her toddler years is an important part of your parenting career. It's up to you to create a safe environment for her. It's up to you to care for her when she's ill. It's also up to you to guide her toward eating the good foods and getting the rest she needs for optimal health.

As you already know, parenting provides lots of challenges. Your reward for meeting these challenges is your child's well-being and love.

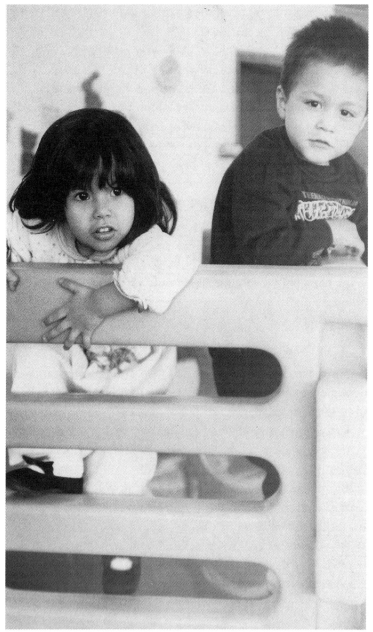

Both boys and girls need to be protected from abuse.

11

Protecting Your Child From Sexual Abuse

- **Teen Parents and Sexual Abuse**
- **Sexual Abuse Is Devastating**
- **Protecting Your Child from Abuse**
- **Heart to Heart Program**
- **Does Abuse Affect One's Parenting?**
- **"I Finally Told My Mom"**
- **Who Do You Tell?**
- **Getting Professional Help**

When I was 3, I was molested, and when I was 10 I was raped by my mother's boyfriend. Sometimes I find myself getting frustrated real easily because I have a lot of flashbacks. On Saturday I had a real bad flashback, and it hurts Dorian's dad to see me go through that.

My boyfriend was the first person I told. Then I finally told my mom. I didn't speak up sooner because I thought my family would turn on me, and they did. They blamed me.

I finally told my mom's boyfriend, when I was 11, "Stop, don't touch me. Get away from

*me." Other than that I think he would have continued
it for years.*

*I'm learning to be more honest now because I feel
like there's a big weight lifted from my shoulders. So
many girls have gone through it, especially those in
parenting classes.*

Denae, 16 - Dorian, 11 months

Teen Parents and Sexual Abuse

*I was sexually abused by my brother. My mother
doesn't know. I was only like 3 or 4, and I remember
all these things that my brother used to do to me. Now
I'm getting on with my life. I don't talk to my brother.
People say you're lucky, you have boys and you don't
have to worry about that. But you do.*

Kerrianne, 19 - Sergy, 3; Leonardo, 4

Many teen mothers have been sexually abused. In fact,
according to research, a majority have faced some degree
of abuse as they were growing up. Abuse happens to boys,
too, and teen fathers have been abused.

*Sexual abuse happened to my husband. My hus-
band never said anything until he was older, and then
nobody believed him. It happened when he was 6, and
he talked about it when he was 12.*

*Doug told me he thought I wouldn't like him
because of what happened to him. I told him I love
him for who he is, not for what somebody did to him.*

I don't know how to protect Caelin.

Alaina, 17 - Caelin, 4 months

Victims of sexual abuse are likely to blame themselves.
The child feels violated, but s/he may not tell anyone. The
abuser usually either tells them, "This is our little secret,"
or threatens harm to them or their family if they tell.

Sexual Abuse Is Devastating

Kaye was molested by her grandfather when she was very young. Then, when she was 14, her sister-in-law's brother raped her. She commented:

It is the most devastating thing. My sister-in-law still doesn't understand, and it was her brother who was the minister who raped me. She still sees it as sex, but it is not sex when I was 14 and he was 28. Just the devastation, the damage it does, they do not understand at all. Even my husband at times doesn't understand. He wants me to be sexual with him. "Why do you have these hang-ups?"

It's very hard to understand unless you have been through it. I look at it as murder. Sexual abuse takes some things you can never get back. It takes so much away from you, and piece by piece you have to try to get it back if you can.

Kaye, 25 - Wade, 11; Dirk, 8; Tanya, 5

Protecting Your Children from Abuse

When I give Karena a bath, I say, "These are your private parts and you don't let anybody touch them. If somebody does, please tell Mommy. You won't get in trouble, and Mommy needs to know."

You need to let the child know she can come to her mother for anything. She can tell mother if something bad happens.

If kids have secure feelings basically, that's a big protection.

Yoko, 25 - Sheila, 9; Matthew, 6; Karena, 2

Whether or not you've been abused, you want to do all you can to protect your child, whether a girl or a boy. One in four females and about one in seven males in the United

States will be sexually abused or raped before age 20. The majority of those committing the abuse are known to their victims.

Some women sexually abuse children, but most of the time the abusers are males. He could be a stranger, but he's more likely to be someone the child knows. He may be a friend of the family, an uncle, cousin, stepfather, mom's boyfriend, or even the biological father.

We often tell children, "Don't talk to strangers." This doesn't take care of the problem since the abuser may have a close relationship with the child.

Some children are taught that adults are always right. They are to respect adults and obey them. Yet no one, adult or child, is always right. And there are adults who are not worthy of a child's respect. Your child needs to know s/he has the right to say "No" to another person, whatever their age.

When you're discussing good touch and bad touch with your children, use concrete examples. Petting your kitty is a good touch. If the cat scratches you, that's a bad touch. If someone you like very much gives you a hug, that's a good touch. However, if you get a funny feeling about that hug, maybe it's a bad touch. Or if your uncle gives you a hug, and that feels good, but he does something else that feels different, is that a good touch or a bad touch?

Children can understand the difference between good touch and bad touch. You might add that sometimes a doctor may need to examine them, but in that case, you should be there with them. A good doctor welcomes a parent being there during a child's physical examination.

An important point you make with your children is that they can talk to you about anything. They should never feel embarrassed or ashamed when they talk to you.

Teach them the correct names for body parts. If they

don't think they should say the words penis and vagina,
how can they tell you somebody asked them to touch it?

No one should force affection on a child. Your child has
a right to say "No," even when grandpa wants to kiss her or
tickle her. Grandpa may be hurt, but you can help him
understand that today Jessica doesn't feel like being hugged
or tickled. Jessica needs to know, no matter how little she
is, that she doesn't hug or kiss anyone unless she wants to.

Heart to Heart Program

A couple of years after her first son was born, Kaye
participated in the Heart to Heart Program. This program,
developed by the Ounce of Prevention Fund based in
Chicago, teaches teen parents how they can protect themselves and their children from sexual abuse. Kaye
explained:

> *Heart to Heart helped me learn how to protect my
> children. It made me deal with my own sexual abuse. I
> was walking around with blinders on just like my
> mom. I learned so much from that program, and I
> brought it home to the kids.*
>
> *My son was 2 when I went through Heart to Heart.
> I think the key thing is to talk about abuse. It's not a
> taboo thing, something you talk about only in secret.
> We talk openly and freely.*
>
> *The same way you say "Don't touch that stove, it's
> hot," you say "Don't let anybody touch your body."
> They need to know that somebody they love can hurt
> them.*
>
> *When I was growing up it was like it would be
> somebody jumping out of an alley, but that wasn't the
> way it was. It could be your father, your grandfather,
> your uncles. Children need the information to protect*

*themselves in that family setting instead of always
hearing about people off the street.*

*Even at this age I think they understand between
good touches and bad touches. They are affectionate
with others in the family.*

*My daughter is good at speaking up. Somebody will
come up to her and say, "Give me a hug, give me a
kiss," and she will say "No," and that's all right. You
have to respect children's wishes.*

*A lot of times sexual abuse happens because the
child needs attention. That's not what they want, but
it's like the child who is abused physically. He will
still love that person anyway because it's some kind of
attention.*

*I'm still very very concerned about my grandfather.
Other kids are over there but my kids aren't at all.
And that hurts because I would like my kids to have a
relationship with my grandmother.*

Kaye

Does Abuse Affect One's Parenting?

Kaye talked about the lingering effects of her abuse. Her
sons are now 11 and 8, and her daughter is 5. In spite of her
efforts to go on with her life, she says the abuse has made
a difference.

First, she explained that her first pregnancy, when she
was 13, was very much because of the abuse. She had not
been allowed to make decisions about her own sexuality.
She was not a real partner in what was happening. So one
day she made a choice, and had sex with the boy across the
street. She conceived, and, in spite of her family's horror at
the pregnancy, for her it was a positive thing:

*From the very beginning I accepted my pregnancy.
I needed that baby, and the pregnancy stopped the*

*abuse for awhile. Pretty much it kept me safe. I had
begun to feel very worthless, very abnormal, low self-
esteem. I felt very misused. Having that baby made me
feel loved again and made me feel like I had a pur-
pose in life. So I welcomed the pregnancy.*

Kaye also talked about the negative effects her abuse has
had on her parenting.

*At times I feel like I'm not as physical with my kids.
With my boys, I hug and I kiss them, but sometimes I
push them away because I don't want any sexual
overtones there. I have more freedom with my daughter. When my boys want to sit on my lap, I can't deal
with it. Even at times, bathing them when they were
little, I was real uncomfortable. I think that's the
negative.*

*Sometimes I can push them away when I feel like
it's too much. But they need the affection just as much
as my daughter does. I put a space between us, and I
wish that wasn't there.*

To parent a child well, a parent needs to feel secure and
have high self-esteem. In studies of victims of sexual
abuse, the victims score low on self-worth. They have a
higher rate of depression, and of drug and alcohol abuse.

If the parent can't feel good about her/himself, it will be
difficult to raise a child with good self-esteem. You can't
give someone something you don't have.

"I Finally Told My Mom"

*You need to talk about it. First you need to be
honest with yourself. Recognize that it did happen.
You have to be real with yourself. I was going off the
handle. For sanity's sake you have to tell somebody.*

Denae

If this has happened to you, are you talking to someone about your experiences? Too often, sexual abuse is suffered in silence. It's considered a taboo subject, yet the abuser, if not reported, will most likely continue by abusing someone else. Victims wonder if their stories would be believed. Or they don't want to disrupt family relationships.

I finally told my mom about my grandfather because I couldn't stand it happening any more.

My mother took this very hard. She almost had a nervous breakdown. This made her deal with her own abuse. My grandfather had sexually abused her when she was a child, too. She had a lot of guilt that if she had exposed him way back then he wouldn't have had the opportunity to get to me.

Kaye

Dealing with a daughter's (or son's) sexual abuse is, of course, difficult for a mother. She may blame herself, as Kaye's mother did, because she had not shared the nightmare of her own sexual abuse. In other families, the mother may have known about the abuse, or at least the victim thinks she did. Then why didn't Mom protect her? Denae continues to wonder:

I have a lot of hard feelings toward my mom. Until recently she was visiting her boyfriend in jail, yet he confessed to all of this (abuse). I started going to therapy once he turned himself in. I can't afford to freak out because it would be Dorian who would suffer.

Denae

Who Do You Tell?

If you've been abused and you haven't gotten help, haven't talked to anyone about it, you'd probably be wise to talk to someone. If you can't talk to your mother, start with a friend, an aunt, perhaps a counselor at school. Find somebody you can trust.

You need to find someone who really understands the dynamics of abuse, and that *the abuse was not your fault.* Kaye discovered sometimes the conversation would turn around to "What did you do?" She said:

> *If someone puts the blame on you, know absolutely it's not your fault. After my grandfather was arrested, the police officer told me that even if a prostitute stands out in the street naked, nobody has the right to touch her unless she permits it. That helped me a lot.*
>
> Kaye

Getting Professional Help

Because an abused person generally has so many questions and doubts, s/he may need to find professional help. It's important to find a counselor who understands the dynamics of sexual abuse, how it can affect other aspects of your life, especially your parenting.

If you don't know who to call in your area, call the Sexual Assault Crisis Agency for Victims hotline, 562/597-2002. Someone there should be able to refer you to a counselor and/or suggest where to go for help in your area. Also, in many states, according to Jan Stanton, director of Heart to Heart, the YWCA and the YMCA provide help for sexual abuse victims.

If none of these sources help, call the Ounce of Prevention's Heart to Heart Program in Chicago, 312/922-3863, and ask where to go in your area for the help you need.

Whether you're trying to recover from the abuse you've endured, or you're determined to protect your child from abuse — or both — you have an important task. *More power to you!*

A satisfying partnership takes lots of love, respect, and caring.

12

The Partnership Challenge

- **Parenting Alone**
- **Will You Love Again?**
- **Is Marriage a Solution?**
- **Divorce Is Difficult**
- **Making the Marriage Decision**
- **Making a Good Partnership Better**
- **Winning Over the Other Parents**
- **Planning Your Family**
- **What Are Your Options?**
- **Enough Time for First Child**

I'm still young, I want to have friends, and I'd like to go out. It's frustrating for Nathan, too, because rarely do we go out by ourselves.

Things change. I used to say, "Oh, I'm so in love." I still love him, but . . . I'm stressed sometimes so much that it's, "Oh, what do you want?"

Before I got pregnant, I thought everything would be so easy — the baby is so cute, and we're a little family, but it's not quite that way.

We're trying to keep our relationship going, but I feel so far away from him. He works

*4 a.m.-1 p.m., then sleeps until 8 or 9. Then he gets
up, but I'm tired and I go to bed. But we both realize
Dakota needs two parents.*

Zandra, 16 - Dakota, 11 months

*Usually we stay home with Dakota. We get out once in
awhile, not often. That hurts our relationship because
Zandra likes to go out.*

*Sometimes it seems like we're drifting apart. We don't
see each other much. About the only time I see Zandra is
when I pick her up at school.*

Nathan, 20 - Dakota, 11 months

Parenting Alone

Many teenage mothers are rearing their toddlers alone.
The baby's father may have vanished when he learned the
young woman was pregnant. Or they may have stayed
together throughout pregnancy, perhaps longer, then ended
their relationship.

If you're parenting alone, you're probably working very
hard and, if you're like many other single parents, you'd
rather be sharing your parenting responsibilities.

If you're with your baby's other parent, however, or with
a different partner, you probably face some problems in
parenting together. Good relationships take time, effort, and
energy in addition to love just as good parenting takes time,
effort, and energy in addition to lots of love.

It's hard to parent alone, but it's also difficult to fit in
enough time and effort for both your partner and your
child. Making good decisions concerning partners is perhaps one of the hardest issues faced by teenage parents.
There is likely to be even more heartbreak in a failed
relationship when there is a child involved.

Teenage parents of toddlers tend to be involved in a

variety of relationships. Only one in five teenage mothers is married when her child is born. By the time the child is three, a high percentage of these marriages have ended. By this time, many teenage parents are with a different partner.

Will You Love Again?

I'm very cautious with the guys I go out with. If he doesn't like Chandler, even if he's the nicest guy in the world, it's good-bye.

Gretchen, 17 - Chandler, 13 months

Sometimes a single teenage mother may wonder if she will ever have a love relationship again. If a man knows she has a child, will he want to be with her? Or will she be left alone to parent her child? If he does see her, will their new relationship upset her child? Elysha is typical of many teen mothers who say this isn't a problem for them:

My having a child doesn't bother anyone. I had thought a lot of young men would think, "Well, you have a child so I won't bother." But a lot of the guys I know are attached to Antoine.

"Can Antoine come with us?" they ask. Sometimes we include him.

The only time I date are the weekends. I work eight hours a day, then pick up my child at school. We do what we have to do at home, we go to bed, and then we start the day again.

Elysha, 21 - Antoine, 4

Sometimes it's hard for a toddler to understand why mom leaves her to go out with her boyfriend:

When a boyfriend comes to pick me up, Susie decides she wants to go. She puts her clothes on and follows me out to the car. We try to explain, "Mommy

is going out, and you have to stay home. "
My mom usually picks Susie up and brings her in
the house. She cries until she realizes Mom will come
home later. Then she goes to bed.

Cathi, 18 - Susie, 34 months

If Cathi talked with Susie ahead of time about her plans
for the evening, Susie might be more accepting. Perhaps
Cathi could do something special with Susie before she
goes out. If Cathi's date means she won't be able to read
Susie a bedtime story, perhaps they could have a reading
session earlier in the day.

Shalimar is pleased that her friend Pete makes a special
effort to include Ellie in their plans:

It makes me feel better, because if Ellie didn't like
the person I'm dating, I'd have a problem.
The first time she saw Pete kiss me, she said,
"Don't kiss my mom. "
Pete said, "Ellie, I love your mom, too. I like both
you and your mom, and I want to be with you both. "
Then he gave her a hug good-bye, and she kissed him.

Shalimar, 19 - Ellie, 30 months

Is Marriage a Solution?

Some parenting couples stay together, but choose not to
marry during pregnancy, or perhaps not for months or even
years after their baby is born. Many of these young couples
live together. At first, they are likely to be with his parents
or hers because they can't afford a place of their own. By
the time their child is a toddler, they may have their own
apartment.

However, Rosemarie's parents insisted she and Dick
marry immediately after they learned the young couple was
pregnant. Rosemarie and Dick lived with Rosemarie's

parents for a year. Their relationship didn't go well, and
they were delighted when they were finally able to get an
apartment by themselves.

Like many other teenage couples, Rosemarie and Dick
thought moving out on their own would solve their
problems. This didn't happen:

> *Moving out didn't solve our problems. We were*
> *fighting more and more.*
>
> *Then one day Dick hit me, and that did it. My*
> *father used to knock us around when I was little, and*
> *I vowed that when I grew up, nobody was going to hit*
> *me. I had warned Dick I'd leave if he ever hit me.*
> *So I did.*
>
> Rosemarie, 19 - Helen, 3

Sadly, violence is a part of many teenage (and older)
relationships. It takes a great deal of courage for a woman
to walk out of such a relationship, especially if she has no
money and no place to go. Rosemarie at least had a high
school education and some job skills. She continued
her story:

> *To be perfectly honest, right after my divorce, I*
> *didn't know how we would survive. But I didn't have*
> *a choice. I couldn't live with him. Now I'm trying*
> *to put my life back together, and I'm adjusting*
> *pretty well.*
>
> *Helen and I are living with my sister and her*
> *husband and their baby. We can't afford a decent*
> *apartment by ourselves, so I split living expenses with*
> *them. I couldn't handle living with my parents now*
> *because they would try to take over. Being with my*
> *sister is a little different because we're peers.*
>
> Rosemarie

If you're in an abusive relationship, do everything you can to get out of it. *You don't deserve to be hit!* Check the phone book or ask your school counselor or your social worker for information about women's shelters in your area, shelters which take women and children.

You might find reading *Breaking Free from Partner Abuse* by Mary Marecek helpful. (See Appendix.) Included are vignettes of women in abusive relationships together with suggestions for escaping such a relationship.

Divorce Is Difficult

For some married couples, divorce may be the best solution to a lot of unhappiness. Divorce is seldom easy, however.

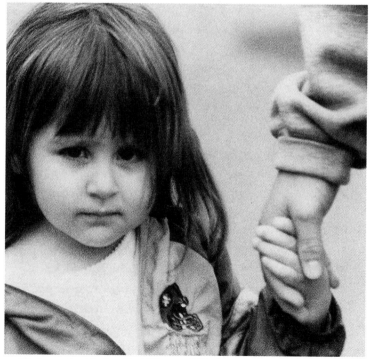

It's important to her that Mom and Dad have a good relationship.

Sometimes marriage counseling *before* divorce can help a couple work through their problems. Divorce is seldom easy for either partner, and it's almost always hard on the children involved. Divorce doesn't solve problems. It's the people involved who must solve those problems. For some, divorce may be a necessary step, but it won't be easy.

Making the Marriage Decision

Whether you've never been married, or you're divorced, you may be considering marriage now. If you are, you and your partner may want to discuss such things as:

- Do you both want to spend the rest of your life together?
- Is one of you working and earning enough to support your family? If only one is working, is s/he willing to support the other one and your child?
- Do you have a place to live? For most couples, it's harder to develop a good relationship while you're living with other people.
- Do your answers agree on such important questions as:
  - When will you have your next child?
  - Will either or both of you continue going to school?
  - Who is expected to have a job? Husband? Wife? Both?
  - Who will take primary responsibility for the care of your child?

You can think of a lot of other things you need to discuss thoroughly before you decide to spend the rest of your lives together.

Trust is an important factor in a good relationship. Many young people, not yet quite sure of their own worth, have

problems with jealousy. If he's out without her, he must
have a girlfriend. If she's out with her girlfriends, he's sure
she's getting in trouble. Domingo talked about this issue:

> *I feel trust is the #1 thing you need in a relation-*
> *ship. If you feel you can't trust your significant other,*
> *you should just get out of the relationship.*
>
> *I feel I can talk to Lupe. Some of my friends ask me*
> *why I "let" her go hang out with her friends. And she*
> *trusts me. My friends also say, "Oh, I don't ask her (if*
> *I can go out) because she would never let me. I just go*
> *out." We have time away from each other, and we*
> *don't have to ask why or what.*
>
> *It's really a negative effect on the relationship if a*
> *guy can't trust his girl or a girl can't trust her man.*
> *You can't share your money with someone unless you*
> *trust each other. It has to work both ways.*
>
> *You trust this person to help raise your kid. You*
> *trust this person to help feed you. You always have to*
> *be able to count on this person.*
>
> *Some people say they trust their girl, but when she*
> *takes off for the mall, he asks her, "Who did you see?*
> *What did you do?" That sours the whole thing.*
>
> *I see a lot of jealousy. It's sad. It's not the right*
> *feeling to have in a relationship. If you trust some-*
> *body you shouldn't have no jealousy. You develop*
> *that trust. You want to trust your kid to behave right,*
> *and you want to have that trust in your child's*
> *mother. It's a sad issue not to trust somebody.*
>
> Domingo, 22 - Lorenzo, 4

The two of you might like to read *Teenage Couples:
Caring, Commitment and Change* and *Teenage Couples:
Coping with Reality* (Lindsay) together. You'll find a lot of
suggestions for making a partnership work, whether you're

married or simply living with your partner.

At the back of *Caring, Commitment and Change* is a "Score Card" for teenage marriage decisions. You and your partner might each like to take this "test," then compare your answers. It might help you see more clearly the areas in which you agree and those in which you disagree.

A fairly long questionnaire concerning attitudes toward marriage and living together is in *Coping with Reality*. Completing the questionnaire together is also an excellent way to help you start talking about some important issues. Too often, partners don't communicate well about money, children, families, home preferences, career goals, and other vitally important topics.

Making a Good Partnership Better

It was hard because he went to work, and we both went to school, but on the weekends we would talk. If something bothers us, we talk about it and go from there.

Me and my parents didn't have much communication, and neither did his parents before they got divorced. We decided talking about things was better than arguing about it and just getting mad.

Alaina, 17 - Caelin, 4 months

The relationship with your partner may be more complicated because you're a parent. If it's a poor relationship, you may, because of your child, not feel free to leave. If your partner is not your child's father, you may worry about the effect this situation will have on your toddler.

If you're with a partner, you probably would like your relationship to be as good as possible. One thing to remember is that it's important that neither partner feel put down or badly treated by the other.

Sometimes people talk about a good relationship being a 50-50 situation — each partner has equal rights and responsibilities. A better percentage is probably 60-60 — each partner goes more than half way to please the other. At the same time, each partner needs to realize how important s/he is, and be willing to guard his/her own self-esteem while doing more than his/her share in maintaining a loving and caring relationship with the partner.

> *No matter how bad things get or how hard, we have to do our best to keep our family together. We have to think about Buchanan. We want to raise him the right way with a mother and a father, so we have committed to each other that we are going to be together.*
>
> *When we get in fights . . . like before when we'd fight, one of us would say, "Well, I'm going to leave you." But we made an agreement that when we get angry with each other, we aren't going to say that.*
>
> *We agree that if one of us is angry, we'll show love. We'll say, "Come here, baby, let me hug you."*
>
> Camelia, 16 - Buchanan, 6 months

Maintaining a good relationship is not easy. It takes a lot of nurturing, but, for many, it is worth the effort. Living within a good partnership can make parenting even more satisfying.

Winning Over the Other Parents

When you and your partner have a child together, getting along with the other grandparents is usually important, both for your child and for your peace of mind. Whether or not you live with your partner's parents, you probably want your child to be able to enjoy his grandparents. Sometimes those grandparents need to be won over:

*When she learned I was pregnant, Stan's mother
told him not to see me again, to give the baby up and
go into the Marines as he had planned. "Don't let her
interfere," she told him.*

*The first time I saw Stan's mom was at the hospital
because she didn't want her neighbors to know I was
pregnant. She didn't want her family to know, and she
didn't want her church to know. She wanted me to
stay out of sight.*

*Stan and I decided to get married a couple of
months after Ryan was born. His mother tried to plan
our wedding. I think the closest we ever came to
splitting was when I put my foot down and said, "If
you want to plan this wedding with your mother, then
marry your mother. If you want to marry me, we'll
plan it together."*

Kristin, 23 - Ryan, 8; Tiana, 4

Kristin, however, decided she wouldn't accept a poor
relationship with her husband's parents. They needed to get
along for Ryan's sake, so she took the lead in improving
family relationships:

*Things started changing after I began taking Ryan
over there. I got along good with Stan's brothers and
sisters, so I'd pick a time when they'd be home. I
would act like it was a normal visit to grandma and
grandpa. Then Stan started going along with me.*

*I didn't want to explain to Ryan why grandma
didn't come to visit. I didn't want him to think
grandma didn't come over because she didn't love
him. I didn't want him to think grandma didn't like me
because I got pregnant with him. So I acted normal,
and in the long run, it worked. She respects me.*

Nobody wins if you stay away. I don't know how I

knew that would be best, but I knew it would be wrong to drive a bigger wedge, and I didn't want to come between Stan and his mom.

Kristin

Encouraging positive contact between your child and both sets of grandparents usually is best for the child and for the grandparents. Kristin won over her husband's parents because she was willing to make an effort. At the time, it would have been easier to say, "They don't like me and I don't like them. That's all there is to it." Instead, she was determined that Ryan would win. In the process, everyone in this family became winners.

Whether you're still living with your parents or you're in your own home, fostering a good relationship between your child and his grandparents is important.

Planning Your Family

If you want to be an independent person, you can't depend on the man to use birth control. Independence is important to me — it always has been. If you use birth control yourself, you know for sure.

Darla, 17 - Janis, 2

A lot of teenagers who have one child have another within one or two years. Often this second pregnancy is not planned. It may, in fact, create a real hardship for the young mother:

I didn't want Kerry — it was a total accident. I was on the pill, but I ran out and was going to wait until after my period. This pregnancy upset me terribly. Amy was the only one I wanted. I don't like having two kids. I thought about abortion, but I knew deep down I wouldn't do it.

*Both you and your child are more likely to have the life you want
if you don't have your second child too quickly.*

*Her father's mom said, "But that's my first grand-
child," and my mom said, "You won't be welcome in
the family if you do that." That's my whole family.*
Leslie, 20 - Amy, 27 months; Kerry, 4 months

What Are Your Options?

*Once you're pregnant, it's up to you if you have an
abortion or keep it. I don't put anybody down for an
abortion, because if you know you won't be happy
with that child, it's even more tragic to try to raise it.*

*After she has her baby, every girl should find a
birth control method. I think if I get pregnant again, it
will be because I want to. If you're in a relationship
with one person, both of you should take the
responsibility.*

With one child, I can go ahead and do what I want.

*With two or three children and no husband, I'd be
really limited. I don't want another child until
I'm married.*

Shirley, 20 - Virginia, 4

If you aren't pregnant now, you have three options as far
as pregnancy is concerned. One is obvious. If you don't
have sex, you won't get pregnant. The majority of high
school students still choose this method. If you see statistics
stating that 25 percent of all 15-year-old girls have had
sexual intercourse, that means that 75 percent have not.

Your second option is to use birth control if you're
having sexual intercourse. If you don't want another baby,
this is essential.

*I have a girlfriend who doesn't use birth control
because she says she can't talk about it with her
boyfriend. I tell her if she's too embarrassed to talk to
him, don't have sex with him. The whole idea is
just silly.*

Melinda, 15 - Robin, 9 months

Lots of teenagers think, "It won't happen to me. I won't
get pregnant." But one couple in 25 will become pregnant
at the time of first intercourse. Of the couples having
intercourse twelve times without using contraception, *one-
half* will become pregnant.

Would you ride in a car if you knew that one-half of
those who take twelve rides will have a serious accident? If
you aren't ready to have a baby, or if you already have one
and aren't ready for another, an unplanned pregnancy is
certainly a "serious accident."

You'll find a description of the various methods of birth
control in *Your Pregnancy and Newborn Journey.*

Your third option is to get pregnant. If you're having sex

and you don't use birth control, this is the option you apparently have chosen.

If you're pregnant now, you still have two options other than raising the child yourself. You can get an abortion, or you can release your child for adoption.

Releasing her child for adoption used to be the accepted "solution" for a pregnant teenager who was not married. Today, however, less than four percent of unmarried pregnant adolescents choose adoption for their child. Yet this could be the most loving, caring decision a birthmother could make. For more information on adoption and for personal accounts of young mothers who chose this option, see Lindsay's *Pregnant? Adoption is an Option.*

Enough Time for First Child

Many young mothers and fathers want to have enough time between their babies to give each child the love and attention he needs. They also realize the expense of having one child, and prefer to wait at least two or three years before having another baby.

There are many reasons to delay your second baby, practical reasons like how will you afford another child? One of the most caring reasons is that you want to have enough time and energy to give your first child the attention he needs. Many young parents feel a toddler is better off being an only child for at least two or three years.

Parenting a child or several children is a wonderful experience. It will be more wonderful if you have the resources — time, money, relationship — that you need to parent well. *Your child and your future children will thank you.*

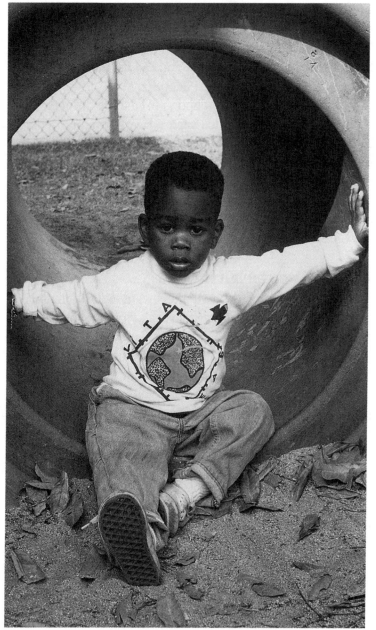

"I don't want to put my son's life in jeopardy."

13

Gang Involvement Versus Parenting

- **Pregnancy May Be a Way Out**
- **Does Gang Involvement Affect Parenting?**
- **Why Join a Gang?**
- **Gang Clothes on Babies?**
- **Will Your Child Join a Gang?**
- **Getting Out**

I've had guns pulled on me and that wasn't much fun, One time me and Lupe and my son were crossing the street, just walking home from the local park. A car cut us off as we were walking, and I was so upset I flipped the driver off. He decided to come back, himself and two women. He ended up pulling a gun on me. Lupe was pushing my son's stroller, and he was no older than 6 months.

Lupe broke into tears crying, "Don't shoot him," and I had nothing to say, it was such a shock. The girls in the car kept telling him to get back in the car, and he finally left.

*I thought I'd keep my temper from here on. Some-
one else might react even more. I put my son's life in
jeopardy.*

*Before, when I was in a gang, I could take off
running and not worry about leaving anybody behind.
In this instance, I couldn't just leave.*

Domingo, 22 - Lorenzo, 4

*Where I used to live there are more gangs than
anything else. There's nothing to do over there for
younger people so gangs are especially important. If
you had money you could hang around with the
football players and stuff, but if you didn't have
money, the gangs were there. I also had a bad
childhood and I was angry a lot.*

*Getting out — it was like little by little. Someone
real close to me died, and I was there and I saw it. It
woke me up in a lot of ways because I had thought it
was all fun and games. I just didn't think beyond what
I was doing. It was like a reality check.*

*Some people don't get out of the gang because
they're too scared. I knew it wouldn't be easy. I was
afraid, but I'd confront people before they confronted
me. My boyfriend didn't know me when I was
like that.*

*Moving away gave me a chance to get my head
straight. I knew girls who have their babies. They're
still over there gang-banging and beating up people
for what they wear, but they're not real mothers.*

*I'm glad I got out of that gang stuff before Dakota
was born. I had one friend over there, a guy, and he
had a little girl. He was in the wrong place at the
wrong time, and they shot her, killed his little girl,
by mistake.*

Zandra, 16 - Dakota, 11 months

Pregnancy May Be a Way Out

*A lot of my girlfriends, when they got pregnant,
said, "This isn't for me." I think some of my friends
got pregnant because they wanted out of the gang.
Most of their boyfriends are still in the gang, and they
aren't helping the girls support the kid.*

*I tell my little sister, if you get in a gang, we're
packing ourselves up and moving. Because when you
need something, they aren't going to be there for you.
When you need someone to talk to, they're just going
to laugh at you and walk away.*

Bridget, 18 - Barnaby, 6 months

Thousands of young people across the country belong to
gangs. They may join, be jumped in, before they reach their
teens. They join a gang because they want to belong to
something. They want to be part of a group. The support
members give each other can be positive. They may feel
protected from other gangs.

Gang membership also may mean involvement with
alcohol, drugs, stealing, involuntary sex, and violence.
Gang violence is often reported in the newspapers, and
gang members speak of seeing friends killed. Many schools
are not safe for students because of gang activity.

Kelsey considered the gang her family. When her mother
died, her homeboys and homegirls all went to her mom's
funeral. "They kind of supported me," she explained. She
moved in with her stepfather, who was gone on the weekends. The house became the hangout for the gang. After
Kamie was born, however, Kelsey realized something had
to change:

*After I had my daughter I started calming down,
and my lifestyle changed. I'm tired of people saying,
"The gang is my family. They're there for me when*

*my other family isn't." That's not even true. They're
there if you have a place to party or if you can get
drugs. We had the house, we had the drugs, we had
the girls. They could come Friday night and Saturday
night and leave Sunday.*

*They were my friends, but where were they when
we got kicked out of the house, where were they when
I needed my mom? When I needed money? The guys,
the partying, all that looks good, but after a while,
you start looking and say, "What are they really
doing for you?"*

Kelsey, 19 - Kamie, 21 months

Lucas and Kelsey are living together now, and Lucas
works full-time. He, too, used to be in a gang:

*Before, I would blow off and go down the street
and look for somebody to beat up. That was me and I
didn't care. But now I have my daughter, and I have
to set an example for her.*

*I started in 7th and 8th grades, and when I got to my
freshman year, I didn't care. I was all into it. But I
still got good grades. I'd always do my homework,
because I still had dreams.*

*I didn't want to be at the same place doing the
same things every day. I didn't want to be in jail, I
didn't want to be strung out on drugs, on the corner
asking for money.*

*Maybe it was seeing what my mom had to go
through. We always were so poor. People would ask
me what we had for dinner, and I didn't want to say
beans and rice. And then my brother, I always saw
him incarcerated, in and out. I decided this had to
stop now in our family.*

Lucas, 21 - Kamie, 21 months

Does Gang Involvement Affect Parenting?

If a gang member becomes pregnant, or is the father of a child, will involvement in the gang have any effect on their child? Is it possible to be a good parent at the same time he is actively involved with a gang? Riley doesn't think so:

I have been to meetings with gang members and they'd bring their kids. They'd be running around listening to what we said. We have all our guns, walking around, drinking, playing with the other kids, smoking weed, and the homeboys, the fathers, don't care. But at the time you don't really think about it because it's not your kids.

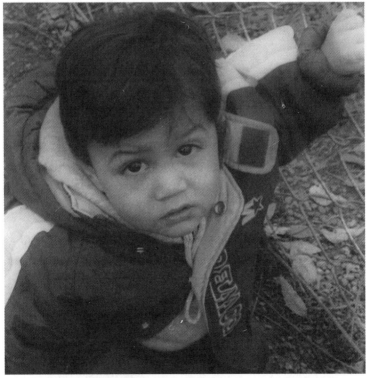

"Now I can't just think of myself, I have my son to think of."

*If I pounded somebody's face in, or I hit him with
something, or he's in the hospital or I left him there to
die, just because he's from a different neighborhood, I
looked and thought, this is somebody's baby even if he
is my age.*

*I looked at my son and thought, will he be like me?
I thought, I might lose my son because of gang violence. My whole family is involved in the gang, my
mother, my father, my uncles. I thought to myself,
things have to change. Dorian is the next generation.
He's the one who's going to school to learn, not be on
the outside doing something wrong.*

*Now I can't just think of myself, I have my son to
think of. I have a beautiful baby, and he needs a lot of
love. When I don't have a job I feel so bad, and I
come close to thinking of going out there and robbing,
selling drugs, but things always come through. I like
my new lifestyle now. I go to work, and I bring a
pretty good sized paycheck home. Everything is going
well right now, and we're getting married next year.*

                                        Riley, 18 - Dorian, 11 months

Sometimes within the gang a toddler is treated like a pet
or a toy. Gang members may give little thought to his needs
or even his safety. The love and nurturing the child needs
may be hard to get.

Gangs vary a great deal, so it's hard to generalize. Many
young people, however, decide parenthood is a reason to
leave. Sheleen explained why she's no longer with
her gang:

*I realized I wasn't getting anywhere, doing things
like that. It wasn't helping me in any way, just being
with my friends. I walked away from all those people.
I told them I have to take care of my son.*

> *My baby's father was in the gang, and he's in jail*
> *now. I don't want anything to do with him.*
> *I wouldn't want Brandt to join a gang when he's*
> *older. There's a lot of bad things that can happen to*
> *him, doing stuff like that. He could get killed.*
>
> Sheleen, 15 - Brandt, 1

Some people walk away from their gang without big problems. Others face being jumped out. Theo explained her situation:

> *When I realized I was pregnant I stopped doing*
> *crazy things. I stopped stealing and doing setups*
> *because I was pregnant. When Nicklaus was four*
> *months old I called my homeboys, and I said, "I*
> *want out."*
> *We were at Mousey's house, and they jumped me*
> *out. They took me in the other room and got my face*
> *bad. My baby didn't hear me crying or yelling, but it*
> *was like he was scared. They brought him out five*
> *minutes after. When they brought him out, he didn't*
> *say anything, it was like he sensed that I was sad. It*
> *was like a "Are you OK?" kind of look.*
> *I don't want my son to be like that at all. I don't*
> *even want him to wear baggy jeans or ever shave his*
> *head, or have anything to do with violence.*
>
> Theo, 19 - Nicklaus, 9 months

Theo realizes now that, if this was something she had to do, it would have been far better to leave Nicklaus with her mother or a friend during this time. Babies and gangs don't mix well. In fact, even a very young baby is affected deeply by the violence around him.

> *It's not a good thing for people to hurt other people*
> *when they're around their babies. People should*

*realize that their babies are going to remember it for
the rest of their lives.*

Francella, 19 - 7 months pregnant

When a gang member decides to leave, it's probably
wise to assure members s/he is not rejecting them. S/he just
can't handle the action or take the risks anymore. It's
usually not necessary to reject them as people, as relatives,
or even as friends.

Why Join a Gang?

*You get involved in the gangs for the affection, for
the love, you get involved for the power, you get
involved because of the territory. You realize you
have a lot of back-up when you open your mouth. You
take a chance, and it doesn't matter until that chance
gets caught up with you.*

Lonnie, 16 - 8 months pregnant

Several young people explained their reasons for joining
a gang. Generally, they felt their own family wasn't there
for them. Dad may have been gone for as long as they can
remember. Mom may have been too busy trying to keep
the family together, and didn't have time or energy left
for them.

*Why do kids join gangs? Maybe they aren't getting
enough attention from their families and they want to
be with their friends. Maybe they have no one to talk
to, no one that's like them and wants to do the things
they want to do.*

*Why did I join? I thought it was fun, going out with
my friends. I don't know, it was just the thing to do. I
think if I had not been pregnant I would still be in it.*

I think parents of a child should not be in a gang. If

If he gets plenty of attention from his parents,
he's less likely to choose the gang life.

you're in a gang you can have a lot of enemies, and
people don't really care if you're with your baby.
They may want to start something. If girls don't like
my friend (who's in a gang), they really don't care if
she has her baby with her.

Sheleen

The poverty may be overwhelming. In some areas, few
activities are available for young people, and the gang
appears to fill that need.

When you're in an area that doesn't have money,
and people are mad and frustrated, it's more likely
to happen.
I feel like I only joined the gang for attention. My
mom was always working, and she's not the kind of
person who shows her feelings. She was just there. I

think if I would have gotten the attention I needed, I wouldn't have looked somewhere else. The gang was like a second family.

A lot of kids feel this way, that nobody else is there for them. I think people who get out of it kind of just grew up. It's not a way of life. It's a sad way of life.

That's why I'm going to get an education. I'm not going to depend on someone else to support me.

Zandra

Riley is quoted earlier in this chapter. He says, *"I thought to myself things have to change. My son is the next generation."* His partner explained why she thinks Riley had joined a gang:

Riley grew up without a father. His dad used to beat on his mom. His dad has been in and out of prison. His stepdad is off and on with drugs, so Riley has never had a strong male role model. He felt dumb because kids would make fun of him. He wanted friends real bad, so he got jumped into a gang.

He never got out of the gang. He just stopped hanging around. You don't owe them an explanation. You just move on with your life.

We both want what's best for Dorian. We want him to have what we didn't have, a good home, with a stable relationship.

Denae, 16 - Dorian, 11 months

Gang Clothes on Babies?

I don't agree with gang clothes on babies. I don't agree with shaved heads on babies. If you want to cut their hair, do that cute little bowl haircut. When they bald their heads, it doesn't look proper, it's not cute. They're babies.

Samantha, 16 - Kaylie, 20 months

He doesn't need to wear gang clothes.

Babies and toddlers tend to be charming little people who generally look good no matter what they're wearing. Most parents, however, enjoy dressing their children as attractively as possible. Many parents like their children to dress somewhat as they do. A toddler on a farm, for example, might wear overalls or jeans most of the time. A child living on the beach may wear a swimsuit the same color as her mother's. Another toddler's shirt may match his dad's.

Small children love to mimic their parents, and they usually think it's great if they're wearing clothes similar to mom's or dad's.

Does this extend to gang attire? The young parents we interviewed don't think so.

*I believe the way you dress is the way you carry
yourself. People who dress their kids in gang clothes,
it's not right. It's true, you get stereotyped whether
it's right or not. And I don't want somebody to come
by and shoot them because of what they wear. There
are sick people out there. A guy in my block got shot
because he was wearing a red hat.*

Kerrianne, 19 - Sergy, 3; Leonardo, 4

Sergy and Leonardo's father continued the discussion:

*I try not to dress my kids like gang people. I don't
want them to be judged because of the way they're
dressed. The way you dress kids is an indication of
how you want them to grow up.*

*In our society clothes make a difference. I have
noticed a lot of people, just because they're dressed in
baggy clothes, they're thought of as gang members.*

*As you get older, common sense will tell you the
gang is not getting you anywhere. Those kids are not
going to put food on your table or a roof over
your head.*

Glen, 25 - Sergy, 3; Leonardo, 4

Will Your Child Join a Gang?

*When I first got pregnant, it was like yes, I'm
pregnant, no big deal. But when I got my sonogram
and I saw this person, then I started thinking. Do I
want people saying, "Your son is in a gang" or "Your
son shot my son"? I thought, I still have a chance.*

Vivienne, 19 - Trevor, 2

About half of the 54 young parents interviewed for this
edition of this book had belonged to a gang. Most were no
longer involved. Not one father or one mother told me s/he
wanted her/his son or daughter in a gang.

They talked about strategies which might prevent their child from going this route. They stressed the importance of staying involved with one's child, of "being there" for that child.

They talked about their parents who were too busy or too poor to support them in school or community activities, and of the difference being involved in sports, for example, might have made in their lives:

We want Dakota in sports. I believe the coach will teach the children the right way, teach them discipline, to be on time, to work hard. I noticed a difference when I was in sports and when I wasn't. When I was in sports, I got to meet a lot more people, and school became more interesting.

You have to keep up your grades, and when I was keeping up my grades, I was learning more. When I wasn't in sports, I stayed home and watched TV. The road didn't seem to be going anywhere. I was just there.

Nathan, 20 - Dakota, 11 months

They also talked a lot about love, and of the importance of expressing that love to their child.

I think the basic thing in raising a child is love. I think he'll get far in life if he knows he can always come home and have a good home-cooked meal with his family. And he won't need to go looking for a gang or be out on the streets because he'll be secure in himself.

I've seen a lot of parents say, "My daughter is in a gang. I give up." If they could just say to that daughter, "I love you." Three little words could change so much.

Camelia, 16 - Buchanan, 6 months

The relationship you build with your child is the most important factor in protecting him from gangs and violence. For more on this subject, see "Teaching Your Child to Be Non-Violent," chapter 10, *Discipline from Birth to Three.*

Getting Out

Some gangs make it extremely difficult for a member to get out. If you're in that situation, and you'd like to change your lifestyle, have you considered leaving your neighborhood? For some people, that appears to be the best solution. It's also likely to be an extremely difficult decision. Even if you'd like to leave, where would you go?

Is there a relative or close family friend who might take you in? Is an older sibling thinking of moving out, and might take you along? How about getting a roommate or other couple to move out of the area with you? Even a few miles away can make all the difference.

If you have no resources, and neither your parents, your relatives, your partner, or your friends can/will help you, you need to go elsewhere for help. Chief of Police Richard Tefank, Buena Park, California, commented, "Getting out takes trying to get some help. If you want to leave the neighborhood bad enough, I think you can.

"That can mean contacting local churches. At least you'd get some support there, and if you need to talk to somebody, it's a good place to go.

"Next, I'd try Child Protective Services. You go there and say, 'I want to get out of this environment with my child. Who could help me?' You aren't going as a Protective Services client. You're going there to seek help, and you might get a supportive social worker who might think, 'I'll help this person because if I don't, they may become my client.'

"I would also suggest contacting law enforcement

because they're always aware of a lot of resources. If you don't have financial resources, no family support, it's going to be tough."

You might also find help by contacting some of the other helping resources listed in chapter 14.

Lonnie had an extensive history of arrests, incarceration, placement in a series of foster homes. Only when she became pregnant did she change her life. She moved back in with her mother, and for the first time in many years, developed a good relationship with her. Lonnie went back to school, even won an achievement award from a local philanthropic organization. She credits her teacher and her mother with helping her, but most of all, she credits a detective in her community:

> *I was supposed to get busted because I left the foster home. One of the detectives who had busted me when I was real young, I think saw through me from the very beginning. I think he saw me as something more than a wanna-be.*
>
> *When he came to my friend's house to look for me, he said, "I know there is something more, and I need to give you a chance to find that something."*
>
> *When he told me that, it kind of made sense. Then after I got pregnant, he talked to my mom. To this day, ever since he told me that, I haven't messed up. I want to give back to society. To me, he was kind of like a guardian angel. I talk to him all the time. He calls to check up on me.*
>
> Lonnie

Help *is* available, but you may have to work hard at finding the help you need to enable you to have the life you want for you and your child. *You and your child are worth the effort!*

Graduating is an important gift to yourself and your child.

14

Your Future — Your Child's Future

- **Looking Ahead**
- **Taking Financial Responsibility**
- **Importance of Education**
- **Non-traditional Jobs**
- **After High School, What?**
- **Job Aids Self-Esteem**
- **Who Stays Home**
- **Heavy Expense of Moving Out**
- **Money Versus Happiness**
- **Other Problems**
- **Finding Community Resources**
- **Writing Life Script**

Being a young mother, I missed out on a lot of things. I dropped out in junior high. When I went back, my friends were graduating. But I finished, and I'm working full-time now.

I'm planning to go to college next year. I love my daughter, and I enjoy being a mother — but a baby is not like a baby doll. You can't put it in the corner while you go out and party. You have to change your world around.

Madge, 18 - Destiny, 3

I feel old compared to when I was first pregnant. I look at life

*differently. I have two children, so I can't just go
around not knowing what I want to do with my life.
I'm more responsible now, and every minute counts.*

*I work and I go to school. I'm not influenced by my
friends like I used to be. Some people, even though
they have children, go on with their lives as if their
parents are going to take care of the child.*

*It doesn't work that way with me. On both sides our
parents don't take the responsibility of raising our
kids. I think it's good they don't. If they did, I would
be taking it for granted and leaving them with my
parents all the time.*

Mary, 21 - Shawna, 4; Ahmud, 20 months

*I stayed in school. You got to go to school so you
can get the kind of job you want. I'm not on welfare
—never was. When paycheck time comes around, I'm
out of money, but I'm getting there. It's being
independent that counts.*

*I want to be an administrative secretary, so I'll be
going to junior college for the next two years.*

Ginger, 18 - Sean, 17 months

Looking Ahead

Your child may be three soon. What kind of future are
you planning for him and for yourself? If you're with his
other parent, are you following your dreams of a satisfying
life together? Are you already an independent family, or on
your way to becoming independent?

If you're by yourself or with another partner, what are
your plans for your future? Are you able to support your
child if you need to do so? If you aren't to that point, what
are you doing now to get there? Are you still in school? Are
you learning job skills? Whether you're your child's

mother or father, it's essential that you be able to support yourself and your child.

Even if she's married, the girl should get a job and learn to be independent, especially the way so many are getting divorced today. If she never knew anything, dropped out of school because she got pregnant, and got married, the only thing she's learning is cleaning and cooking. Beyond that, she doesn't know much if she doesn't ever get a job.

I didn't feel good about myself at first when I knew I was pregnant. Later, I thought of the way I was, and I decided I didn't want Janis to grow up the way I did.

I had to change a lot of my attitudes and think what I wanted to do to change myself.

So often the mother is going to support the child. I like to work because it makes me feel more independent. I don't have to rely on anybody else.

Darla, 17 - Janis, 2

Taking Financial Responsibility

I was working a construction job, making just a little over minimum wage. I thought, "Here we are, bringing a child into the world, and I'm going to have to support the child." I told the construction crew I was going to be a dad, and I wanted some advice.

"Leave now," they told me.

And "Get an abortion."

I hung in there, and when Francene was born, we had benefits so the medical bills were paid. But so much else was on my mind. Will I be able to afford food? The bills? The responsibilities never end.

I was worried about being a father. How do you fill a father's shoes, someone who's supposed to have all

*the answers? How do you live up to a father's
reputation?*

Julio, 24 - Francene, 4; Alina, 3; Gloria, 1

Some teenage fathers and mothers aren't supporting their
child because they're still in school. Others have dropped
out, but can't find a good job. The best approach for them
is to stay in or go back to school and/or get job training to
prepare themselves for supporting their family.

Julio had a low-paying job and, like many other young
fathers, wondered how he could possibly support his
family.

Whether you're the mother or the father, you need to live
up to a parenting "reputation," as Julio says. You'll never
have all the answers — none of us do — but you'll need to
be responsible for your child. Being responsible includes
being financially responsible.

> *I thought it was going to be all easy. I thought I
> was going to coast through it (parenting). I've had a
> lot of hard times, times when I was broke and won-
> dered how my son was going to eat, get diapers. I
> usually found a job, not enough money for myself, but
> enough so my son would have what he needed.*
>
> *My plan before Dorian was born, before I even
> thought about having a baby, was to go to college and
> be an architect, but I got sidetracked. I'm still going
> to college.*
>
> *Now I'm working as a custom plasterer. The pay is
> pretty good, but for a life-time career, no.*
>
> Riley, 18 - Dorian, 11 months

Importance of Education

> *I went back to school because I have to graduate
> for my son. Barnaby's dad didn't graduate, so I'm the*

*one that has to. How would I give my son help when
he comes home and does his math? I had to go back
to school.*

Bridget, 18 - Barnaby, 6 months

Women who achieve at least a high school education are
only half as likely to live in households receiving TANF
(Temporary Aid to Needy Families) as are women who
never graduated. If the young mother depends on welfare
payments, there is never enough money. Now, with welfare
reform, eligibility for help from welfare is severely limited.

*When I moved in with my husband, I stopped going
to school. I went back after Buchanan was born
because I started thinking. I want to get a good job. I
want to have a college education. I want to show
Buchanan that I've done good with my life. I want to
get a job so I can help support him financially as well
as emotionally.*

Camelia, 16 - Buchanan, 6 months

Sharon, too, decided to return to school:

*I'd been out of school for two years. I saw some-
thing at the store about this school for teen parents. I
wrote down the number, went home, and called. I'm
back in school now, and they take care of my kids.*

*I need an education for my kids so I can get a good
job. If my kids want to ask me something, I want to be
able to answer them. I want the best for them. My
husband wants me in school, too.*

Sharon, 19 - Ricardo, 35 months; Monique, 16 months

Sharon is lucky. She lives in a school district which
provides childcare for students' infants and toddlers.

If your school doesn't have a childcare center, and you
don't have a relative or friend who will care for your child

while you continue school, what will you do? See *Your Baby's First Year* for tips on choosing suitable day care for your child and suggestions on handling the expense of that care.

Non-Traditional Jobs for Women

I dropped out of school when I was five months pregnant with Celeste. Then, when I got pregnant again, my sister found out about the Teen Parent Program and said I should go.

I said, "I'm not going. They'll put me down for having a second kid when I'm so young."

But they didn't, and everybody understands where I'm coming from.

I don't want another baby for awhile. I want to have a career. I want to be a mechanic, although my father wants me to think of something else. Our Community College waives fees for single parents.

Noelle-Marie, 19 - Celeste, 2 1/2; Carrie, 9 months

Noelle-Marie's desire to be a mechanic could be a smart choice. Teen parents need jobs that pay family-supporting wages. High-paying jobs for high school graduates are usually in the technical fields, or in occupations considered non-traditional for women.

Jobs and careers traditionally dominated by men tend to pay higher wages and salaries than those traditionally held by women, even when the education required for "male" and "female" occupations is similar. Samples of non-traditional occupations are the technical trades of carpenter, plumber, auto/diesel technician, law enforcement, fire fighting.

If you are a young mother and your parents, like Noelle-Marie's father, don't like the idea of you becoming a mechanic or a plumber, research comparative pay of various kinds of work. Also figure out what it will cost you and your child to live as you would like to live. A non-traditional career could be the route to a more satisfying lifestyle for you and your family.

> *Most of my friends who have had a baby have dropped out of school. It bothers me a lot. Two of my good friends who dropped out will be working at fast-food places or a store, and that's not going to support their children.*
>
> *I don't know if I'll be with my baby's dad forever, and I don't want to have to depend on his income. I want to be able to live on my own.*
>
> Lyra, 18 - Leah, 2 1/2

After High School, What?

Often it's important not to put off getting your education. If you've already graduated from high school, you may decide to go ahead with further training as soon as possible.

Shirley graduated from high school three years ago when Virginia was fourteen months old. Because she had learned office skills in high school, Shirley started working for the county in the welfare department a few months later. After working directly with people applying for welfare, she has some firm opinions on the subject:

> *You don't get anywhere on welfare. I hear people saying, "I have these two children who are starving and. . ." All I can say is, if you care for yourself as a person and for those children, you'll go out there and work. I could never get what I want waiting for a check on the first and the fifteenth. I couldn't live off what somebody else gives me just because I have a*

baby. I want a lot of things for me and my daughter.

Shirley, 20 - Virginia, 4

Remember, if you complete high school, your chances of being on welfare are half what they are if you drop out before you graduate.

Parents, fathers as well as mothers, who continue their education and hold good jobs obviously are much better off

His parents are working hard to give him a good life.

than are parents who quit school and whose only income is
their TANF (temporary) grant.

*First I want to get my GED and start moving on,
then train with computers. I worry about the future a
little. I don't want to be real old and still making
minimum wage. I want to be financially secure.*

Miguel, 20 - Genny, 18 months

Job Helps Self-Esteem

Many young parents also discussed the difference a job
can make in the way they feel about themselves. They often
mentioned that when a mother thinks well of herself, when
she has good self-esteem, she's a better mother than she is
when she's unhappy with herself.

*When Martha was little, we stayed by ourselves for
almost a year. I was home most of the time, watching
TV and being bored. At that time, I wasn't helping
myself. I was depending on my parents plus welfare.*

*Now I'm self-supporting. I feel good about myself
because I'm doing it on my own. I've found out I can
cope, and I love my job. I'm a nurse's assistant, and
I'm taking a medical terminology class.*

I think I'm a better mother when I like myself.

Alta, 22 - Martha, 6; Howard, 3

Of course this applies to fathers, also. Many young men
have difficulty finding a job which pays enough to support
their family. Whether you're a mother or a father, the
importance of workforce preparation cannot be over-
emphasized.

Have you already dropped out of school? Now, this
minute, is the time to return. You can go back to your
regular school or to a special class for teen parents — if

there is such a school in your area.

In most states, if you're 18 or older, you can go to a local community college to take classes to help you earn your high school diploma. Check community college catalogs for job training facilities. Possibilities may include Regional Occupation Programs (ROP) and high school career centers.

You may find help with child care or transportation, especially if you qualify for TANF. Talk to your social worker.

Who Stays Home with the Kids?

If you're with a partner, both of you may need to work simply to be able to pay your bills. Or one of you may decide to stay home with your child(ren) while the other one keeps a job.

In traditional families, the mother stays home and takes care of the children and cleans the house. If they can afford it, many families still prefer to have a parent home while the children are young. Either the mother or the father can care for the children, and either the mother or father can support the family. More often today, however, parents share both roles.

Heavy Expense of Moving Out

Living with your own parents is often difficult when you have a child yourself. Wanting to move into a place of one's own is certainly an understandable goal. If you've never lived on your own, if your parents have always paid the bills, you may not realize how expensive it is to keep an apartment.

I plan to move out in three months when Holly (friend with a baby) turns 18. I'm 15. Hopefully I can

get $350 from welfare. An apartment will be $500 a
month, and I'll split that with Holly. Then we can go
half on the groceries, and Robin will be eating table
food by then. We should be able to make it.

Melinda, 15 - Robin, 9 months

First, it is doubtful that Melinda will be able to receive
welfare if she moves out at age 15. In most states, a mother
under 18 must live with her parents in order to qualify for
TANF. If Melinda can get money on her own, she and
Holly may still have trouble renting an apartment. Apartment owners often choose not to rent to young single
mothers and their children, especially if they must rely on
welfare for their income.

Second, Melinda doesn't appear to be planning realisti-
cally for her other expenses. She and Holly need to talk to
other young families who live on their own. What do they
actually spend for food? What about transportation?
Clothing? Emergency expenses?

The high cost of living independently may be unreal to
you. Or that high cost may be the biggest reason you're still
with your parents.

Money versus Happiness

Money doesn't buy happiness, but the lack of "enough"
money can certainly cause a great deal of unhappiness. As
you plan your future, it's important that you plan how
you'll earn enough money to support your child.

Even if the two parents are together and both are
working, they may have heavy financial problems:

We had credit, and we got deeper and deeper in
debt. When we finally wrote it down in black and
white, we had $2600 debts each month, but we
brought in only $1900.

We wrote letters, trying to be rational. That didn't help. They picked up all our furniture, and we filed for bankruptcy a year ago.

It was hard on the kids when the furniture went. We had no refrigerator. We slept on the floor on a mattress and ate out of an icebox. How do you explain that to kids?

After filing for bankruptcy, your credit is ruined for seven to ten years. You have to get a co-signer or have a lot of collateral in order to get credit.

We scrimp from week to week. We're just not money managers at all. What we're trying now is for Denver to hold the checkbook. He keeps it so I can't write checks.

The worst thing you can do is to file for bankruptcy. I would sell everything in my house before I'd do that again.

I would go to a credit counselor, but Denver won't go. He thinks we should be able to manage it ourselves — but we're not.

It's just that hard. The important thing is to manage your money. I think we should be teaching money management in the schools.

Mitzi, 22 - Selene, 5; Vaughn, 2

Whatever your income, you might think about Mitzi's last comment. Sometimes a class in money management can help a person plan how best to budget her income. If you think you're heading for financial trouble, get help. Don't coast along until you have the big money problems facing Mitzi, Denver, and their children.

You may be able to find a non-profit group offering credit counseling in your community. Be careful of credit counselors who charge big fees.

Look under "Debt Counseling" or a similar heading in your telephone directory. Try to find someone who, at little or no charge, will help you work out a plan to budget your income.

With some professional help, plus lots of effort on your part, you may be able to pull out of seemingly hopeless money problems.

When You Have Other Problems

Of course not all problems come with dollar signs. Teen parents, like everyone else, have ups and downs in their lives.

You may already be in school or you may have a job. You may be making plans for your future and for your child's future.

If, however, your life is not going the way you want it to go, have you considered getting extra help? You don't have to handle everything by yourself.

It's hard being a single parent. We were living together for awhile, and I miss the emotional support.

When I get really uptight, I put Juanita in the crib and let her cry. There's nothing I can do unless I hold her all day, and then I'm more upset.

Esperanza, 17 - Juanita, 12 months

If you're having more problems than you can handle by yourself, the first step is to accept the fact that you need help. Some people find it very hard to admit they aren't making it on their own.

You're probably already getting informal help. Families often are a good source of support. So are friends. In fact, other young parents can offer tremendous support simply because they're facing some of the same problems that are bothering you.

Finding Community Resources

You may need help beyond what your family and friends can give. Perhaps they can suggest community resources for you to contact. Inquire about resources from other people with whom you interact — the director of a childcare center, your minister, doctor, or teacher.

Also check your telephone book. Your county or state Mental Health Association and Psychology Department at your local college may recommend counseling services.

If you're receiving TANF (welfare), ask to see a social worker when you need special help. Social workers often have far too heavy case loads, but some are able to provide extra help to their clients. If you have a local community center, the social worker there may be able to tell you where to go for help with your problems. Your hospital social service department may be a good resource.

More than 300 agencies in the United States are connected with the Family Service Association of America. These agencies offer individual and family counseling at low cost, as well as a variety of other family services.

For the agency in your area, check your telephone directory under the following listings: Family Service Association, Council for Community Services, County Department of Health, Counseling Clinic, Mental Health Clinic, or United Way.

Don't Give Up

Generally you can get a list of hot lines from your telephone operator. Call Information (411 or your area code + 555-1212), then say, "I have this type of problem. Can you help me?"

You may find, as you call hot lines and other community services, that phone numbers you have been given are not helping you. Too often the number has been changed, your call is answered by a recording, or the person responding tells you that agency can't help you.

When this happens, don't give up. If a person answers your call but can't help, ask for referrals. Tell him/her you need help. You don't know where to call next. Explain how much you would appreciate any ideas s/he may give you.

Pregnancy and Marital Counseling

If you're pregnant unexpectedly, your community probably has several agencies specifically organized to help you and others in your situation. Call the Planned Parenthood Association, Florence Crittenton Services, Catholic Charities, or family or children's services. Or talk to your guidance counselor, your doctor, or your pastor.

If you are a single parent, find out if there is a support group for single parents in your community. Check with the above resources for information about such groups. In some areas, Children's Home Society sponsors single parent support groups.

Marriage and family counselors are usually listed in the telephone yellow pages. Your community may have a cost-free counseling agency, or the cost may be based on your income. If you have very little income, you may not be charged a fee.

Independence and self-sufficiency are wonderful things — if they work. All of us need extra help at some time. If this is your time of special need, do whatever necessary to get that help. Both you and your child will be glad you did.

Writing Your Life Script

You get tired, but you can work, you can go to school, you can be with your child. You just have to work it into your schedule.

Brynn, 17 - Brent, 17 months

Some people feel that a young woman who has a child when she is 16 is doomed to a life of poverty and unhappiness. They point out that the young mother will probably drop out of school and won't be able to find a steady job, a job which pays enough to provide for herself and her child. She may feel she has to get married. Her life choices seem quite limited.

If a teenage parent can, however, continue her education, improve her vocational skills, find a job, and, when she is ready, marry someone she wants to marry, her life script (life plan) can be quite different.

Most of the young parents in this book are not settling for a life of hardship because of early childbearing. Instead, many are continuing their education and are acquiring job skills. They are not accepting a life script filled with poverty and unhappiness. They *are* finding that "writing" — and living — a successful life script is a difficult task.

Even very young parents can be in charge of their life scripts . . . if they continue their education and acquire vocational skills. For most young parents, this will be very difficult, but well worth the effort.

You and your child deserve the best there is. If you get your education and improve your vocational skills, you can be in charge of your life script.

More power to you!

Appendix

About the Author

Jeanne Warren Lindsay is the author of sixteen books for and about pregnant and parenting teens. Half a million copies of her books have been sold.

Lindsay's books deal with teenage pregnancy, parenting, adoption from the birthfamily's perspective, and teen relationships. Her *Teen Dads: Rights, Responsibilities and Joys* was selected by the American Library Association as a Recommended Book for Reluctant Young Adult Readers.

Lindsay has worked with hundreds of pregnant and parenting teenagers. She developed the Teen Parent Program at Tracy High School, Cerritos, California, and coordinated the program for many years. Most of her books are written for pregnant and parenting teens, and quotes from interviewees are frequently used to illustrate concepts.

Lindsay grew up on a farm in Kansas. She has lived in the same house in Buena Park, California, for 36 years. She loves to visit the Middle West, but says she's now addicted to life in southern California. She and her husband, Bob, have five children and five grandchildren.

Lindsay is the editor of *PPT Express*, a quarterly newsletter for teachers and others working with pregnant and parenting teens. She speaks frequently at conferences across the country, but says she is happiest while interviewing young people for her books or writing under the big elm tree in her backyard.

Bibliography

The following bibliography contains books of interest to pregnant and parenting teens. Workbooks and other classroom aids are available for some of these titles. The address and phone number of a publisher is listed only with the first resource described.

Prices quoted are from *Books in Print*, 1997-1998. Because prices change so rapidly, however, and because publishers move, call your local library reference department for an updated price and address before ordering a book. If you can't find a book in your bookstore, you can usually get it directly from the publisher. Enclose $3 for shipping per book. See page 223 for an order form for Morning Glory Press publications.

Bjorklund, David F., and Barbara R. Bjorklund. *Parents Book of Discipline*. 1990. 272 pp. $5.95. Ballantine Books.
Emphasizes that discipline is not the same as punishment, but is a fundamental way parents teach their children to respect others and themselves.

Crary, Elizabeth. *365 Wacky, Wonderful Ways to Get Your Children to Do What You Want*. 1995. 102 pp. $9.95. Parenting Press, Inc., P.O. Box 75267, Seattle, WA 98125.

Includes hundreds of positive (and sometimes zany) ideas for solving common problems with young children.

_____. *Love and Limits.* 1994. 48 pp. $6.95. Parenting Press, Inc.
Offers parents lots of useful ideas to help their children behave well.

_____. *Without Spanking or Spoiling: A Practical Approach to Toddler and Preschool Guidance.* 1993. 126 pp. $12.95. Parenting Press, Inc.
Book offers dozens of examples and exercises to guide parents in finding the best methods to suit their family's needs.

Green, Martin I. *A Sigh of Relief: The First-Aid Handbook for Childhood Emergencies.* 1994. 384 pp. $16.95. Bantam Books, 414 East Golf Road, Des Plaines, IL 60016. 312/827-1111.
Lots of illustrations and information. Easy-to-find suggestions for treating childhood emergencies. It's a great resource for teen parent classes.

Heart to Heart Program. For information, contact Jan Stanton, Heart to Heart, Ounce of Prevention Fund, 122 South Michigan Avenue, Ste. 2050, Chicago, IL 60603. 312/922-3863.
An innovative approach to preventing child sexual abuse by teaching teen parents to protect their children from abuse. Program can be implemented in a school or community-based setting. Practitioners participate in a two-day training and purchase the curriculum and facilitator's guide.

Heine, Arthur J. *Surviving After High School: Overcoming Life's Hurdles.* 1996. 244 pp. $14.95. J-Mart Press. P.O. Box 8884, Virginia Beach, VA 23450-8884. 800/487-4060.
Contains an amazing amount of information about independent living— getting and keeping a job, taxes, budgets, shopping, handling a checking account and credit card, housing, transportation, and much more. Excellent information source for teens highly motivated to live on their own.

Lansky, Vicki. *Getting Your Child to Sleep . . . and Back to Sleep.* 1991. 132 pp. $6.95. The Book Peddlers. 15245 Minnetonka Boulevard, Deep Haven, MN 55345-1510. 1-800/255-3379.
Book offers a wealth of suggestions for dealing with babies and small children who don't sleep as regularly as their parents would like.

Leach, Penelope. *Your Baby and Child from Birth to Age Five.* Revised, 1997. 560 pp. $20. Alfred A. Knopf, 400 Hahn Road, Westminster, MD 21157. 800/733-3000.
An absolutely beautiful book packed with information, many color photos

and lovely drawings. Comprehensive, authoritative, and outstandingly sensitive guide to child care and development.

Lerman, Evelyn. *Teen Moms: The Pain and the Promise.* 1997. 192 pp. Paper, $14.95; hardcover, $21.95. Morning Glory Press, 6595 San Haroldo Way, Buena Park, CA 90620. 1-888/612-8254.
Teenage mothers talk to us — to the adults surrounding them who can't decide if these young women are whores, trash to be discarded by society, or if they are victims of hopelessness and helplessness that poverty spawns. Stories from teen moms together with illuminating research.

Lighter, Dawn. *Gentle Discipline: 50 Effective Techniques for Teaching Your Children Good Behavior.* 1995. 107 pp. $6. Meadowbrook Press, 18318 Minnetonka Boulevard, Deephaven, MN 55391.
Author believes teaching children good behavior is much easier, more productive, and more pleasant than focusing on punishing bad behavior.

Lindsay, Jeanne Warren. *Do I Have a Daddy? A Story About a Single-Parent Child.* 1991. 48 pp. Paper, $5.95; hardcover, $12.95. Free study guide. Spanish edition available. Morning Glory Press.
A beautiful book for the child who has never met his/her father. A special sixteen-page section offers suggestions to single mothers.

_____. *School-Age Parents: The Challenge of Three-Generation Living.* 1990. 224 pp. Paper, $10.95; hardcover, $15.95. Teacher's Guide/Study Guide, $2.50 set. Morning Glory Press.
*A much needed book for dealing with the frustrations, problems, and pleasures of three-generation living. Useful for helping teen parents communicate with **their** parents.*

_____. *Teen Dads: Rights, Responsibilities and Joys.* 1993. 192 pp. Paper, $9.95; hardcover, $15.95. Teacher's Guide and Workbook, $2.50 each. Morning Glory Press.
A how-to-parent book especially for teenage fathers. Offers help in parenting from conception to age 3 of the child. Quotes from teen fathers.

_____. *Teenage Couples — Caring, Commitment and Change: How to Build a Relationship that Lasts. Teenage Couples — Coping with Reality: Dealing with Money, In-laws, Babies and Other Details of Daily Life.* 1995. 208, 192 pp. Paper, $9.95 ea.; hardcover, $15.95 ea. Workbooks and curriculum guide available. Morning Glory Press.
Series covers such important topics as communication, handling arguments,

keeping romance alive, sex in a relationship, jealousy, alcohol and drug addiction, partner abuse, and divorce, as well as the practical details of living. Lots of quotes from teenage couples.

_____. ***Your Baby's First Year: A Guide for Teen Parents.*** 1998. 224 pp. Paper, $12.95; hard-cover, $18.95. Morning Glory Press.
Parenting book written especially for teen parents. Reader-friendly. See board game under Smallwood, page 220.

_____ and Jean Brunelli. ***Your Pregnancy and Newborn Journey.*** 1998. 208 pp. Paper, $12.95; hardcover, $18.95; Spanish ed., ***Adolescentes como padres—Jornada de tu embarazo y nacimiento del bebé.*** 1993, 192 pp. Paper, $9.95; hardcover, $15.95. Study guides available. Morning Glory Press.
Prenatal health book for pregnant teenagers. Includes section on care of the newborn and a chapter for fathers. Also available in Easier Reading Edition (third grade reading level) with workbook and teacher's guide (1992 edition). See board game under Smallwood, page 220.

_____ and Sally McCullough. ***Discipline from Birth to Three.*** 1998. 208 pp. Paper, $12.95; hardcover, $18.95. Morning Glory Press.
Provides teenage parents with guidelines to help prevent discipline problems with children and for dealing with problems when they occur.

Marecek, Mary. ***Breaking Free from Partner Abuse.*** 1999. 96 pp. $8.95. Quantity discount. Morning Glory Press.
Lovely edition illustrated by Jami Moffett. Underlying message is that the reader does not deserve to be hit. Simply written.

McCoy, Kathy, and Charles Wibbelsman, M.D. ***The New Teenage Body Book Guide.*** 1992. 288 pp. $15. Berkley Publishing, P.O. Box 506, East Rutherford, NJ 07073. 800/631-8571.
Crammed with information for teenagers about everything from their bodies, changing feelings, teenage beauty, and special medical needs of young adults to sexuality, venereal disease, birth control, pregnancy, parenthood.

MELD Parenting Materials. Nueva Familia: Six books in Spanish and English. ***Baby Is Here. Feeding Your Child, 5 months-2 years. Healthy Child, Sick Child. Safe Child and Emergencies. Baby Grows. Baby Plays.*** 1992. $10 each. MELD, 123 North Third Street, Suite 507, Minneapolis, MN 55401. 612/332-7563.
Very easy to read books full of information. Designed especially for Mexican and Mexican American families, but excellent for anyone with limited

reading skills. Ask MELD for catalog of other materials designed especially for school-age parents.

MELD, published in collaboration with. *The Safe, Self-Confident Child.* 1997. $8.95. MELD.
Important information on how to protect children from harm, and ways to help children improve their self-confidence.

Parent Express Series: *Parent Express: For You and Your Infant. Spanish edition: Noticlas para los padres. Parent Express: For You and Your Toddler.* Each newsletter, 8 pp. $4 each set. ANR Publications, University of California, 6701 San Pablo Avenue, Oakland, CA 94608-1239. 510/642-2431.
Wonderful series of newsletters for parents. The first set, available in English and Spanish, starts two months before delivery and continues monthly through the first year of the child's life. Second set with twelve letters covers second and third years. Good resource for teen parents. Beautiful photos, easy reading.

Pollock, Sudie. *Will the Dollars Stretch? Teen Parents Living on Their Own.* 1996. 96 pp. $6.95. Teacher's Guide, $2.50. Morning Glory.
Four short stories about teen parents moving out on their own. As students read the stories, they will get the feel of poverty as experienced by many teen parents —as they write checks and balance the checkbooks of the young parents involved.

Reynolds, Marilyn. True-to-Life Series from Hamilton High. *Baby Help. Beyond Dreams. But What About Me? Detour for Emmy. Telling. Too Soon for Jeff.* 1993-1998. 160-256 pp. Paper, $8.95 each; hardcover, $15.95 each. Quantity discounts. Morning Glory Press.
Wonderfully gripping stories about situations faced by teens. Start with Detour for Emmy, award-winning novel about a 15-year-old mother. Continue with Too Soon for Jeff, story about a reluctant teen father. Students who read one of Reynolds' novels usually ask for more. Topics cover partner abuse, acquaintance rape, reluctant teen father, sexual molestation, racism, fatal accident, and school failure.

Rodriguez, Luis J. *Always Running — La vida loca: Gang Days in L.A.* 1993. 260 pp. $11. Touchstone, Rockefeller Center, 1230 Avenue of the Americas, New York, NY 10020.
The author tells his own story of gang life in East L.A. in the 70s. It's a vivid memoir that explores the motivations of gang life and cautions against the death and destruction that inevitably claim its participants. Helps reader understand the reasons young people join gangs, and the difficulties of breaking free.

Silberg, Jackie. *Games to Play with Toddlers.* 1993. 286 pp. $14.95. Gryphon House, Inc., P.O. Box 207, Beltsville, MD 20704-0207. 800/638-0928.
Silberg divides games for the first two years into three-month segments and also into categories such as Growing and Learning Games, Kitchen Games, and Special Bonding Games.

Smallwood, Diane, developer. **Games: "Challenge of Toddlers," "Baby's First Year,"** and **"Pregnancy and Newborn Journey."** 1998; 1996; 1996. $29.95 each. Morning Glory Press.
Board games based on Teens Parenting series of books. Combine fun and learning as you play .

Spock, Benjamin, M.D., and Steven J. Parker, M.D. **Dr. Spock's Baby and Child Care.** 1998. 939 pp. $7. Pocket Books, a division of Simon & Schuster Inc., 1230 Avenue of the Americas, New York, NY 10020.
Generations of parents have relied on Dr. Spock's bestseller as their parenting sourcebook. Now updated and expanded.

Stewart, Nancy. **Your Baby from Birth to 18 Months: The Complete Illustrated Guide.** 1997. 192 pp. $15.95. Fisher Books, 4239 W. Ina Road, Suite 101, Tucson, AZ 84741. 520/744-6110.
Provides clear and valid information about caring for the new baby up to age 18 months. Well illustrated.

Williams, Kelly. **Single Mamahood: Advice and Wisdom for the African American Single Mother.** 1998. 190 pp. $12. Carol Publishing Group, 120 Enterprise Avenue, Secaucus, NJ 07094.
Down-to-earth, sister-to-sister guide. Offers suggestions on how to deal with work, school, child support, discipline, dating again, and more.

Wolff, Virginia E. **Make Lemonade.** 1995. 208 pp. $15.95. Henry Holt.
Wonderful novel about teenager living in a Project who takes a job baby-sitting for a teenage mom, and who eventually sees the mom back in school, her children in child care, and her life back on focus.

Wonderley, Stan. **Learning Activities for Infants and Toddlers.** 1998. 248 pp. $22.95. Blue Bird Publishing, 2266 S. Dobson, #275, Mesa, AZ 85202. 602/831-6063.
Simple activities using material commonly found in the home. Can help infants and toddlers develop a wide range of skills.

Index

Adolescence, 34-35
Adoption, 179
Antibiotics, 150
Appetite, 117
Balancing board, 46-47
Bedtime problems, 100-104, 106-109
Bedtime ritual, 99-100
Bilingual, 24-25
Books, non-sexist, 65
Brain development, 30-31
Breaking Free from Partner Abuse, 170
Burns, risk of, 143-144
Car safety, 146-147
Child-proofing, 40
Choices, 38
Colds, 150
Consistency in discipline, 41
Contraception, 178
Counseling, 209-211
Dad, non-biological, 69
Dental care, 152-153

Dependency, 119-120
Diarrhea, 148-149
Divorce, 170
Doll play, 57-59
Dress-up play, 58
Ear infection, 151
Eating, 80-95, 117
Education, importance of, 198
Emotional development, 26, 115-116
Family planning, 176-179
Fast-foods, 83, 91-92
Fathers, involvement of, 66-79, 199-200
Fears, 39-40
Food Pyramid, 82, 91, 95, 117
Future planning, 197-212
Games, 51-52, 129
Gangs, 185-195
Gangs, getting out, 194-195
Gangs, reasons for joining, 188-190
Gatchell, Lois, 13-14
Good touch/bad touch, 158

Grandparents, 93-94, 174-176
Guns, 185
Handedness, 129
Health, 147-152
Heart to Heart Program, 159-160, 163
Helping parent, 59-60
Holidays, celebration of, 131-132
Illness, 141-142, 147-152
Imagination, 56-65, 125, 127, 130-131
Immunizations, 147
Independence, development of, 33-41, 121
Intellectual development, 26-28, 112-115
Jealousy, 172
Job training, 199
Jobs, non-traditional, 202-203
Junk food, 88, 89-90, 91-94
Language, development of, 21, 23-25, 44, 60-63, 112-115, 133, 151
Library, 114-115
Life Script, 211-212
Marecek, Mary, 170
Marriage, 168-173
Money management, 206-208
Music, 58, 59, 126
Negative stage, 33-39
Night waking, 105
Nursing Bottle Syndrome, 30
Nutrition, 82-83, 86-94, 117
Obesity, 86, 90-93
Ounce of Prevention Fund, 159, 163
Painting, 127-128, 136
Partner relationship, 164-179
Play space, 49
Play, 42-55, 124-139
Play, active, 44-48, 137-
Playing ball, 47, 138-139
Poisons, 145-146

Pregnancy, 176-179, 183
Puzzles, 54
Reading, 38, 63-65, 112-115
Routine, 38, 99-100, 109, 120-121, 123
Safety, 141-147
Sand play, 136
Scribbling, 44, 53-54
Self-care, 39, 112
Self-esteem, 25-26
Sex education, 117-118
Sexual abuse, 154-163
Sexual abuse, effect on parenting, 160-161
Sexual Assault Crisis Agency for Victims, 163
Single parent, 68, 166, 167-168
Sleep, 96-109, 116
Smoking, 145
Stanton, Jan, 11-12, 163
Swearing, 61
Swing, 46
Teething, 152-153
Tefank, Richard, 194-195
Television, 132-135
Temper tantrum, 36-37
Temporary Aid to Needy Families (TANF), 201, 204, 205, 206, 209-210
Three-generation living, 93-94
Toilet teaching (training), 40, 118-119
Toys, 21, 46-47, 49-50, 52, 54, 126-127
Toys, made at home, 47, 51-52, 54, 126-127
Toys, storage of, 49-50
Vaporizer, 150
Violence, 133-135
Violence in relationship, 169-170
Walking, 22-23
Water play, 47
Weaning, 28

MORNING GLORY PRESS

6595 San Haroldo Way, Buena Park, CA 90620
714/828-1998; 888/612-8254 — FAX 714/828-2049; 888/327-4362

ORDER FORM — Page 1

Please send me the following:

	Price	Total
Books, Babies and School-Age Parents		
Paper 1-885356-22-6	14.95	_____
— Hardcover 1-885356-21-8	21.95	_____
Organizing TAPP: Useful Forms for Teen Parent		
Programs Paper 1-885356-23-4	4.95	_____
— **Teens Parenting Series:**		
Your Pregnancy and Newborn Journey		
Paper 1-885356-30-7	12.95	_____
— Hardcover 1-885356-29-3	18.95	_____
— Workbook 1-885356-31-5	2.50	_____
— **Board Game** 1-885356-19-6	29.95	_____
— *Your Pregnancy and Newborn Journey —*		
Easier Reading Edition (GL3)(1991 edition)		
Paper 0-930934-61-x	9.95	_____
— Hardcover 0-930934-62-8	15.95	_____
— Workbook 0-930934-63-6	2.50	_____
— Teacher's Guide 0-930934-68-9	2.50	_____
— *Adolescentes como padres*(1991 edition)		
Paper 0-930934-69-5	9.95	_____
— Workbook 0-930934-71-7	2.50	_____
— Teacher's Guide 0-930934-72-5	2.50	_____
— *Your Baby's First Year*		
Paper 1-885356-33-1	12.95	_____
— Hardcover 1-885356-32-3	18.95	_____
— Workbook 1-885356-34-x	2.50	_____
— **Video** 51 min. 1-885356-02-1	195.00	_____
— **Board Game** 1-885356-20-x	29.95	_____
— *The Challenge of Toddlers*		
Paper 1-885356-39-0	12.95	_____
— Hardcover 1-885356-38-2	18.95	_____
— Workbook 1-885356-40-4	2.50	_____
— *Discipline from Birth to Three*		
Paper 1-885356-36-6	12.95	_____
— Hardcover 1-885356-35-8	18.95	_____
— Workbook 1-885356-37-4	2.50	_____
— **Video** 52 min. 0-930934-97-0	195.00	_____
— *Teen Dads: Rights, Responsibilities and Joys*		
Paper 0-930934-78-4	9.95	_____
— Hardcover 0-930934-77-6	15.95	_____
— Workbook 0-930934-79-2	2.50	_____
— Teacher's Guide 0-930934-80-6	2.50	_____
— **Teens Parenting Sample Kit** — 5 books (4 *Teens*		
Parenting titles plus *Teen Dads*),		
5 workbooks, 3 guides,		
2 videos, 2 games	498.00	_____

— **Quanity Discounts Available on Single, Multiple Titles**

Total (Transfer to back page) _____

ORDER FORM — Page 2

			Price	Total
Novels by Marilyn Reynolds:				
—	*Baby Help*	1-885356-27-7	8.95	_____
—	*But What About Me?*	1-885356-10-2	8.95	_____
—	*Too Soon for Jeff*	0-930934-91-1	8.95	_____
—	*Detour for Emmy*	0-930934-76-8	8.95	_____
—	*Telling*	1-885356-03-x	8.95	_____
—	*Beyond Dreams*	1-885356-00-5	8.95	_____

(Hardcover novels, $15.95 each.)

Breaking Free from Partner Abuse
- — Paper 0-930934-74-1 — 8.95 _____
- — *Did My First Mother Love Me?* Paper 0-930934-84-9 — 5.95 _____
- — Hardcover 0-930934-85-7 — 12.95 _____
- — *Do I Have a Daddy?* Paper 0-930934-44-x — 5.95 _____
- — Hardcover 0-930934-45-8 — 12.95 _____
- — *¿Yo tengo papá?* Paper 0-930934-82-2 — 5.95 _____
- — Hardcover 0-930934-83-0 — 12.95 _____

Parents, Pregnant Teens, Adoption Option
- — Paper 0-930934-28-8 — 8.95 _____

Pregnant? Adoption Is an Option.
- — Paper 1-885356-08-0 — 11.95 _____
- — *Surviving Teen Pregnancy* Paper 1-885356-06-4 — 11.95 _____

School-Age Parents: Three-Generation Living
- — Paper 0-930934-36-9 — 10.95 _____

Teen Moms: The Pain and the Promise
- — Paper, 1885356-25-0 — 14.95 _____
- — Hardcover 1-885356-24-2 — 21.95 _____

Teenage Couples: Expectations and Reality
- — Paper 0-930934-98-9 — 14.95 _____
- — Hardcover 0-930934-99-7 — 21.95 _____

— *Caring, Commitment and Change*
- — Paper 0-930934-93-8 — 9.95 _____
- — Hardcover 0-930934-92-x — 15.95 _____

— *Coping with Reality*
- — Paper 0-930934-86-5 — 9.95 _____
- — Hardcover 0-930934-87-3 — 15.95 _____
- — *Will the Dollars Stretch?* Paper 1-885356-12-9 — 6.95 _____
- — Teacher's Guide 1-885356-15-3 — 2.50 _____

TOTAL (Inc. first page) _____

Please add postage: 10% of total—Min., $3.50;
15%, Outside U.S.

California residents add 7.75% sales tax _____

TOTAL _____

Ask about quantity discounts, Teacher, Student Guides.
Prepayment requested. School/library purchase orders accepted.
If not satisfied, return in 15 days for refund.

NAME _____ PHONE_____

ADDRESS _____